CATS' WHISPERS AND TALES

Also by Robert Westall

Fiction
Blitz
Blitzcat
Break of Dark
The Call and Other Stories
If Cats Could Fly
The Cats of Seroster
The Christmas Cat
The Christmas Ghost
The Creature in the Dark
The Devil on the Road
Echoes of War
Falling into Glory
Fathom Five
Fearful Lovers
Futuretrack Five
Ghost Abbey
Ghosts and Journeys
Gulf
The Haunting of Chas McGill
The Kingdom by the Sea
The Machine-Gunners
The Night Mare

Old Man on a Horse
A Place for Me
The Promise
Rachel and the Angel
The Scarecrows
Size Twelve
The Stones of Muncaster Cathedral
Stormsearch
A Time of Fire
Urn Burial
A Walk on the Wild Side
The Watch House
The Wheatstone Pond
The Witness
The Wind Eye
Yaxley's Cat

For adults
Antique Dust

Non-fiction
Children of the Blitz

CATS' WHISPERS AND TALES

Edited by Robert Westall

Illustrated by Kate Aldous

MACMILLAN CHILDREN'S BOOKS

For William Birch with thanks for his help,
and the Birch family cats, Moppet, Tom and Tabitha.

And for Dominique King and her cat Petronella.

R.W.

First published 1996 by Macmillan Children's Books

This edition published 1998 by Macmillan Children's Books
a division of Macmillan Publishers Limited
25 Eccleston Place, London SW1W 9NF
and Basingstoke

Associated companies throughout the world

ISBN 0 330 35257 1

Edited and designed by The Albion Press Ltd,
Spring Hill, Idbury, Oxfordshire OX7 6RU

3 5 7 9 8 6 4 2

A CIP catalogue record for this book is available from the British Library

Printed and bound in Great Britain by Mackays of Chatham plc, Kent

CONTENTS

5

The Enemies of Cats

The Cat and Friendship

The Cat and Domestic Life

Cats and Institutions

The Cat and the Sea

The Cat and Murder

The Cat and War

The Cat and Endings

THE CAT'S PRAYER

BELGIAN TRADITIONAL

O my master,

Do not expect me to be your slave,
  I have a thirst for freedom.

Do not probe my secret thoughts,
  I have a love of mystery.

Do not smother me with caresses,
  I have a preference for reserve.

Do not humiliate me,
  I have a sense of pride.

Do not, I beg, abandon me,
  I have a sure fidelity.

I'll return your love for me,
  I have a sense of true devotion.

INTRODUCTION

VALERIE BIERMAN

T
O BE invited to write an introduction to *Cats' Whispers and Tales* is a singular honour and pleasure – tinged with great sadness. Pleasure, because it was through cats that I enjoyed an all too brief friendship with Bob Westall, and sadness as his untimely death robbed us of one of the finest of writers for young people. His many letters to me were a great joy especially when we shared our thoughts on cats. Bob loved them. "Cats to me are one of life's great and certain plusses. When I get angry with God, I can forgive him because he made cats – a divine and beautiful joke," he wrote in one letter.

Cats were an important part of his life appearing in many of his books. The short story which was the forerunner of his award-winning novel *Blitzcat* appears in this collection entitled *East Doddingham Dinah*, and *Yaxley's Cat*, *Size Twelve*, *The Christmas Cat* and *The Witness*, are amongst the many books that all pay homage to his beloved companions. Several of the stories in this collection are about his own cats – Furble and her kittens in *David and the Kittens*, Vicky the midwife cat who reappears in *Blitzcat*, as old Skinny in a memorable scene when she assists the cat in giving birth before the bombing of Coventry.

During his lifetime Bob had shared his home with some sixty-seven cats and he once wrote to me, "There is no small pleasure in life greater than a litter of kittens in your kitchen drawer. I do love that moment at ten weeks, when they turn adolescent and won't obey their mum any more. It's good to know that adolescence is not confined to humans!"

But his favourite cat was Jeoffrey, whose small size often leads people to think that he is only half-grown. His fur is creamy pink with pale fawny red ears and a ringed tail: Bob considered him to have "silver and pink fur with eyes the colour of pale green grapes!" Jeoffrey is no timid cat, small he may be in size but he has a lion-size personality, ruling the house in which Bob lived, minutely inspecting any visitor who visits his domain. He possesses a face which has an expression of wordly wisdom and canniness – a cross between the Artful Dodger and Chas McGill! Jeoffrey, according to Bob, is a thinking cat who not only studies squirrels in his garden but makes valiant efforts to become one, climbing hand over hand (or paw over paw) to walk precariously along the tops of conifer hedges. By putting his muddy paw prints all over a letter to Bob's editor, he became the inspiration for *A Walk on the Wild Side*, a collection of cat stories. Jeoffrey is a creature of ritual which is described in *Cats' Whispers and Tales*. As I write this introduction, Jeoffrey keeps a watchful eye over the proceedings from a photograph of himself perusing the *Independent* from the comfort of the inside of a paperbag! He is alive and well in his Cheshire home, still trying to outwit the squirrels – but never succeeding.

This anthology was a labour of love for Bob. He took the greatest of pleasure in gathering together his favourite stories and poems. The poetry was firmly aimed at pleasurable pieces. I offered him a couple of poems I'd discovered on the death of a cat but these were politely but firmly declined. "There was a lot of wonderful 'grieving' cat poetry – one could have made a very beautiful, mournful book, but I kept control of myself." This collection celebrates the cat, those creatures who give us so much delight by allowing us to share their lives. And it celebrates the work of one of the greatest of writers, a good friend who loved cats – Robert Westall.

THE CAT IN ITSELF

CATALOGUE

ROSALIE MOORE

Cats sleep fat and walk thin.
Cats, when they sleep, slump;
When they wake, stretch and begin
Over, pulling their ribs in.
Cats walk thin.

Cats wait in a lump,
Jump in a streak.
Cats, when they jump, are sleek
As a grape slipping its skin –
They have technique.
Oh, cats don't creak.
They sneak.

Cats sleep fat.
They spread out comfort underneath them
Like a good mat,
As if they picked the place
And then sat;
You walk around one
As if he were the city hall
After that.

If male,
A cat is apt to sing on a major scale;
This concert is for everybody, this
Is wholesale.
For a baton, he wields a tail.

(He is also found,
When happy, to resound
With an enclosed and private sound.)

A cat condenses.
He pulls in his tail to go under bridges,
And himself to go under fences.
Cats fit
In any size box or kit
And if a large pumpkin grew under one,
He could arch over it.

When everyone else is just ready to go out,
The cat is just ready to come in.
He's not where he's been.
Cats sleep fat and walk thin.

THE DOBERMAN

GRACE FLANDRAU

NOT LONG ago I saw a huge Doberman Pinscher, so fierce that the family later had to get rid of him, bound into a room where the cat dozed on the sofa. He made a furious lunge towards the cat. The latter did not stir, did not stiffen or even hiss. It merely (and rather languidly) opened its eyes. It opened them very wide. The pupils, which had been large and soft, narrowed to a thin perpendicular black line, and it stared without expression into the Doberman's face. I suppose it was sheer surprise that the cat should neither move nor flee which first halted the dog, and the momentary pause was enough. His eyes met those others – so ruthless, so cold, so supremely unflinching, and after a long moment he turned and walked away pretending he hadn't seen the cat at all.

WHY DO CATS KEEP CRYING TO BE LET OUT AND THEN CRY TO BE LET IN AGAIN?

DESMOND MORRIS

CATS HATE doors. Doors simply do not register in the evolutionary story of the cat family. They constantly block patrolling activities and prevent cats from exploring their home range and then returning to their central, secure base at will. Humans often do not understand that a cat needs to make only a brief survey of its territory before returning with all the necessary information about the activities of other cats in the vicinity. It likes to make these tours of inspection at frequent intervals, but does not want to stay outside for very long, unless there has been some special and unexpected change in the condition of the local feline population.

The result of this is an apparent perversity on the part of pet cats. When they are in they want to go out, and when they are out they want to come in. If their owner does not have a small cat-flap on the back door of the house, there will be a regular demand for attention, to assist the cat in its rhythmic territorial supervision. Part of the reason why this repeated checking of the outside world is so important is because of the time-clock message system of the scent-marks. Each time a cat rubs against a landmark in its territory or sprays urine on it, it leaves a personal scent which immediately starts to lose its power. This decline is at a steady rate and can be used by cats to determine how long it has been since the scent-marker rubbed or sprayed. The repeated visits by a cat to inspect its territory are motivated by a need to reactivate its fading scent signals. Once this has been done, comfort and security beckons again, and the anxious feline face appears for the umpteenth time at the window.

CATS AND PSI-TRAILING

ROBERT WESTALL

T HE ABILITY of cats to find their way home over long distances is no longer in scientific dispute. After all, carrier pigeons can do it too. What is far more amazing (and still under dispute) is psi-trailing, that is the power of cats to track their owners down over long distances of unknown territory.

The scientific research has been done by Doctors Joseph Rhine and Sara Feather, of Duke University, North Carolina. Of the hundreds of examples drawn to their attention, only fifty-two have passed their severe research criteria. These included:

1. The stories must be told by the owners themselves.
2. There must be some distinctive mark – a scar or old injury, patterns of the coat.
3. There had to be corroboration by independent witnesses.

With twenty-two cases accepted and on file, Doctors Rhine and Feather are completely satisfied that trips up to 3,000 miles were a genuine phenomenon, and not the result of coincidence and self-delusion.

TERRITORIAL CATS

MARCUS SCHNECK AND JILL CARAVAN

CATS ESTABLISH territories for much the same reasons that humans build or buy homes – to have a safe place of their own for sleeping, eating, defecating and recreation. Like humans, cats are territorial by nature. Even house cats who never go outside have favourite places within the house for their needs, even if it's only a room or a part of a chair. Where several cats live in a house, territories may blur until all residents jointly claim the house and offer mutual defence against others. If your cat is not confined indoors, it will also have a territory outside the house and a social position to go along with it . . . Cats mark their territories by scratching and depositing scents in their urine and faeces or from glands on their bodies. Territories can be as large as 100 acres or more for rural cats and as small as a few feet for house or city cats. In households with more than one cat, territories are sometimes time-shared: one cat gets it in the morning, another in the afternoon. Cats organize themselves into family-type hierarchies in which every cat has a position and follows certain rules. New cats in the neighbourhood must fight to be accepted and win territory. Males are organized by strength. The toughest tom becomes the head of the "family", with power over the other members in the ranks below him. Occasional changes occur in position when one member is overthrown or neutered. Although tom cats rule the biggest area of territory, they do not get priority in courtship. Land, not sex, is what puts them at the top. Females are organized by their motherly accomplishments. The queen with the most kittens is top mama. When queens are neutered, they slide down on the social ladder. Females and neutered males possess only small plots and fight harder than big tom cats to retain their little islands. Cats who own large areas are not as possessive because they have so much territory and are unable to spend enough time protecting it all. But when they decide to fight, they usually win. Amid the private properties there are common grounds for socializing, mating, hunting, or whatever. To reach these places, cats have to follow certain trails so as not to violate other territories or antagonize enemies (like dogs). Some paths are private, but most are common, like human roads.

16

QUORUM PORUM

RUTH PITTER

In a dark garden, by a dreadful tree,
The Druid Toms were met. They numbered three,
Tab Tiger, Demon Black, and Ginger Hate.
Their forms were tense, their eyes were full of fate;
Save the involuntary caudal thrill,
The horror was that they should sit so still.
An hour of ritual silence passed: then low
And marrow-freezing, Ginger moaned "OROW",
Two horrid syllables of hellish lore,
Followed by deeper silence than before.
Another hour, the tabby's turn is come;
Rigid, he rapidly howls "MUM MUM MUM";
Then reassumes his silence like a pall,
Clothed in negation, a dumb oracle.
At the third hour, the black gasps out "AH BLURK!"
Like a lost soul that flounders in the murk;
And the grim ghastly, damned and direful crew
Resumes its voiceless vigilance anew.
The fourth hour passes. Suddenly all three
Chant "WEGGY WEGGY WEGGY" mournfully,
Then stiffly rise, and melt into the shade,
Their Sabbath over, and their demons laid.

Porum; *Genitive plural of "Puss"*

THE CAT'S REPUTATION IN HISTORY

THE CAT IN EGYPT

HERODOTUS (500 B.C.)

THE NUMBER of domestic animals in Egypt is very great, and would be much greater if the increase in cats were not thus prevented. The female cats, when delivered of their young, carefully avoid the company of the males, who to obtain further attention from them, contrive and execute this stratagem. They steal the young from the mother, which they destroy but do not eat. This animal which is very fond of its young, from its desire to have more, again covets the company of the male.

In every accident of fire, the cats seem to be actuated by some supernatural impulse, for the Egyptians surrounding the place which is burning, appear to be occupied by no thought but that of preserving their cats. These, however, by stealing between the legs of the spectators, or by leaping over their heads, endeavour to dart into the flames. The circumstances, whenever it happens, diffuses universal sorrow. In whatever family a cat by accident happens to die, every individual cuts off his eyebrows.

The cats, when dead, are carried to sacred buildings, and after being salted are buried in the city Bubastis.

They who meet to celebrate the festival at Bubastis embark in vessels, a great number of men and women promiscuously mixed. During the passage some of the women strike their tabors, accompanied by men playing on flutes. The rest of both sexes clap their hands, and join in the chorus. Whatever city they approach, the vessels are brought to shore: of the women, some continue their instrumental music, others call aloud to the females of the place, provoke them by injurious language, dance about and indecently throw aside their garments. They do this at every place near which they pass. On their arrival at Bubastis, the feast commences by the sacrifice of many animals, and upon this occasion a greater quantity of wine is consumed than in all the rest of the year. The natives report that at this solemnity, seven hundred thousand men and women assemble, not to mention children.

The number of beasts is comparatively small, but all of them, both those which are wild and those which are domestic, are regarded as sacred. Their laws compel them to cherish animals: a certain number of men and women are appointed to this office, which is esteemed so honourable that it descends in succession from father to son. In the presence of these animals, the inhabitants of the cities perform their vows. They address themselves as supplicants to the divinity, who is supposed to be represented by the animal in whose presence they are. They cut off their children's hair, sometimes the whole of it, sometimes half, sometimes a third part: this they weigh in the balance against a piece of silver: as soon as the silver preponderates, they give it to the woman who keeps the beast, she in turn feeds the beast with pieces of fish which is their constant food. It is a capital offence designedly to kill any one of these animals: to destroy one accidentally is punished by a fine, determined by the priests.

Other nations will not suffer animals to approach the place of their repast: but in Egypt they live promiscuously with the people.

THE LAW OF HYWEL DDA, KING OF SOUTH WALES A.D. 936

WELSH (10TH CENTURY)

THE WORTH of a cat is this — the worth of a kitten from the night it is kittened until it shall open its eyes is one legal penny. And from that time till it shall kill mice, two legal pence. And after it shall kill mice, four legal pence, and so it shall always remain.

The value of a cat which guards a king's barn, if it is killed or stolen: its head is to be put downwards on an even clean floor, and its tail is held up, and wheat is poured about it until the tip of its tail be covered. Unless the grains can be obtained, its value is a sheep with her lamb and wool.

The attributes of a cat and of every animal the milk of which people do not drink, are valued at a third of its worth, or the worth of its litter.

Whoever is to sell a cat is to answer for her not going a caterwauling every moon and that she shall not devour her kittens, and that she shall have ears, teeth and nails, and be a good mouser.

Her duties are to see, to hear and kill mice, to have her claws entire, to rear and not devour her kittens, and if she be so bought and be deficient in any one of these, let one-third of her worth be returned.

THE CAT

GEOFFREY CHAUCER (14TH CENTURY)

Lat take a cat, and fostre hym wel with milk,
And tendre flesh, and make his couche of silk,
And lat hym seen a mous go by the wal;
Anon he weyveth milk, and flesh, and al,
And every deyntee that is in that hous,
Swich appetit hath he to ete a mous.

THERE WAS A PRESBYTERIAN CAT

ANONYMOUS

There was a Presbyterian Cat
Went forth to catch her prey;
She brought a mouse intill the house,
Upon the Sabbath day.
The minister, offended
With such an act profane,
Laid down his book, the cat he took,
And bound her with a chain.

Thou vile malicious creature,
Thou murderer, said he,
Oh do you think to bring to Hell
My holy wife and me?
But be thou well assured
That blood for blood shall pay,
For taking of the mouse's life
Upon the Sabbath Day.

Then he took down his Bible,
And fervently he prayed,
That the great sin the cat had done
Might not on him be laid.
Then forth to execution
Poor Baudrons she was drawn,
And on a tree they hanged her hie
And then they sang a psalm.

POPE INNOCENT VIII ORDERS CAT WORSHIPPERS TO BE BURNT AS WITCHES (15TH CENTURY)

GYLES BRANDRETH

CAT-WORSHIP spread through Europe until, in the fifteenth century, Pope Innocent VIII ordered cat-worshippers to be burned as witches. Not until the late eighteenth century did cats come into their own again.

ST. OSYTH WITCH TRIALS

ENGLISH (16TH CENTURY)

ONE URSULA KEMP was charged with having four familiars "whereof two of them were hes, and the other two were shes; the he spirits were to punish and kill unto death and the two shes were to punish with lameness and other diseases of bodily harm". The two he spirits were Tittey, who appeared in the likeness of a grey cat, and Jac like a black cat. Another one of the accused Alice Manfield, was said to have four imps, Robin, Jack, William and Puppet, two hes and two shes "all like unto black cats".

WITCH'S FAMILIAR

AMERICAN, SALEM (17TH CENTURY)

HE SAID unto her, he believed she was a Witch. Whereat she being dissatisfied said, That some she-Devil would shortly fetch him away! Which words were heard by others, as well as himself. The Night following as he lay in his Bed, there came in at the Window, the likeness of a Cat, which flew upon him, took fast hold of his Throat, lay on him a considerable while, and almost killed him. At length he remembered what Susanna Martin had threatened the Day before; and with much striving he cried out, Avaunt, thou She-Devil! In the name of God the Father, the Son, and the Holy Ghost, Avaunt! Whereupon it left him, leap'd on the floor, and flew out at the Window.

CLEANLINESS

EDWARD TOPSELL (17TH CENTURY)

IT IS a neate and cleanely creature, oftentimes licking hir own body to keep it smooth and faire, having naturally a flexible backe for this purpose. And washing hir face with her fore feet: . . . And her nature is to hide her own dung or excrements, for she knoweth that the savour and presence thereof, will drive away her sport, the little Mouse being able by that stoole to smelle the presence of hir mortall foe.

THE DECEITFUL DOMESTIC

THOMAS PENNANT (18TH CENTURY)

THIS ANIMAL is so well known as to make a description of it unnecessary. It is a useful, but deceitful domestic; active, neat, sedate, intent on its prey. When pleased purres and moves its tail; when angry spits, hisses, and strikes with its foot: when walking, it draws in its claws. It drinks little; is fond of fish: washes its face with its fore-foot, (*Linnaeus* says at the approach of a storm). The female is remarkably salacious: a piteous, squalling, jarring lover. Its eyes shine in the night: its hair when rubbed in the dark emits fire; it is even proverbially tenacious of life: always lights on its feet; is fond of perfumes: Marum, Catmint, Valerian, &c. —

THE POPE'S CAT

CHATEAUBRIAND (19TH CENTURY)

I HAVE as companion a big greyish-red cat with black stripes across it. It was born in the Vatican, in the Raphael loggia. Leo XII brought it up in a fold of his robes where I had often looked at it enviously when the Pope gave me audience . . . it was called "the Pope's cat". In this capacity it used to enjoy the special consideration of the pious ladies. I am trying to make it forget exile, the Sistine Chapel, the sun on Michelangelo's cupola, where it used to walk, far above the earth.

QUEEN VICTORIA

GYLES BRANDRETH

THE RSPCA was founded in 1824. Queen Victoria took a great interest in it, and ordered that a medal, known as the Queen's Medal, should be prepared for presentation to the Society's most notable workers. A design was created and submitted to the Queen, who noticed there was no cat among the animals depicted and directed that a cat should be placed in the foreground of the medal – she even sketched one in the design. She said she felt it was time the Royal Family tried to change the general feeling of aversion to and contempt for cats that then prevailed, and later wrote to the Society, specifically requesting that they should do something for the protection and safety of cats, which were generally misunderstood and badly treated.

THE CAT – MOTHERHOOD AND KITTENHOOD

DAVID AND THE KITTENS

ROBERT WESTALL

THE KITTENS were no more. It was like a death in Gran's house. David sat and swung his legs in the awful silence, and thought how it all began. Was it only three months ago?

"Furble's getting fat," said David.

"Furble's having kittens," said Gran.

"Shall we have to have the vet?" asked David, alarmed.

"Lord love you, no. She'll know what to do. She's a farm-cat born and bred. And a grand ratter. They say good ratters make good mothers."

Furble grew fatter.

"She's shaped like a *pear*," said David.

"She's like a pod," said Gran. "A pod full of peas. Feel. Gently. You can feel all the little heads."

David counted four.

Then suddenly Furble sat up with her front legs splayed and her ears and eyes going every which way.

"They're kicking her," said Gran. David stared at the tiny explosions under Furble's white belly-fur. And the bewilderment on Furble's face.

"Are you sure she'll know what to do?"

"Just you wait," said Gran.

As the days passed, Furble gave up ratting. She just sat and washed and washed her white belly-fur. Bare pink patches began appearing.

"She's wearing her fur away licking," said David.

"That's so the kittens will know where to feed," said Gran. "Look you can see her nipples clear."

When Furble had grown so fat she couldn't *grow* any fatter, Gran got the usual place ready – the bottom drawer of the kitchen cupboard. She lined it with plain paper. "Not newsprint," said Gran. "We don't want newsprint coming off on their fur. I hope she takes to the drawer. Young cats can be so silly their first time. Welly had hers on a shelf ten feet from the ground. We had a rare time searching for them, when she strolled in all skinny one morning."

Furble sat in the shadowed part of the drawer, looking broody. The other she-cats looked in over the top. But one look from Furble was enough to send them away again. She began to pant, and then tried to climb out of the drawer onto Gran's knee.

"They'll have them on your knee, if you let them," said Gran. "If they're fond of you." She put Furble back firmly, but went and sat on the floor by the drawer, and stroked the cat. "They like their humans near."

Then suddenly Furble shuddered and kicked out her back legs backwards, and there was a transparent sausage on the end of a string. With a kitten trapped inside, a struggling, heaving sausage of head and legs, all glistening.

"What do we do?" yelled David.

"Watch," said Gran.

Furble doubled round like a hoop. Her white teeth flashed on the struggling sausage.

"She's killing it. She's eating it," shouted David. "Help."

But the next second the sausage was empty, and a tiny wet mouse-like thing was feebly struggling on the wet paper, towards the bulk of its mother. And Furble's huge tongue was licking it on and helping it. David had never seen anything so weak and helpless.

"Four," said Gran. "I thought there were four. Two little ginger toms, a black tom, and a little white female, I reckon. Anyway, I can guess who the fathers were..."

"Fathers?"

"Four kittens can have four different fathers," said Gran.

Just then Furble got up and leapt out of the drawer, sending squeaking kittens flying in all directions. She flew out of the cat-flap.

"To relieve the calls of nature," said Gran. "But watch the kittens."

Squeaking loudly, the kittens were rolling about the wet paper. Blind, helpless, tiny legs flailing hopelessly. And yet, by some miracle, within a minute they were all back in one tiny squirming heap.

"Why," gasped David. "How?"

"To keep warm, and not to be alone. They're all they know, when their mum's away. And they do it all by hearing each other, because they're blind. Once they're together they're quiet."

The kittens grew, and grew further. Slowly their ears, folded to their skulls, opened like little petals. Behind their slits, the blind eyes bulged and moved. Their tails, from being thin and rat-like, grew into fat little triangles. They lay on an old blanket in the drawer, now. A blanket full of valleys, folds and creases. David had invented a game. As soon as Furble and Gran left the kitchen, he picked up the kittens from their tight wriggling heap, and put one in each corner of the drawer. Immediately, their squeaking started. And then, still blind, by rolling, falling, crawling, paddling along their fat bodies with tiny legs, they found each other again, and the squeaking stopped, and the wriggling of the heap started again.

"Why do they never stop wriggling?"

"To get into the middle where it's warmest. And *don't* pick them up too much, or they'll smell of you, not Furble. Then she might reject them. She might even *kill* them."

David felt guilty.

On the tenth day, Gran said: "Watch their eyes. They should open today. Once their ears are up, their eyelids split."

And by the evening, some kittens had one-and-a-half eyes open, and others no more than a glinting slit.

"Must watch those eyes," said Gran. "This is when wild kittens get eye infections and go blind. See how much Furble is licking their eyes. There's antiseptic in her spit."

But the oddest thing was, once the kittens' eyes were open, they refused to stay in their tight squirming ball, and began endless meandering crawls round the drawer. Just like ants on the patio outside. . . Furble kept picking them up by the scruff of the neck, and putting them back in the heap.

"Now her troubles are starting," said Gran.

It was the black kitten who got out of the drawer first. He'd been trying for ages to claw up the side. Suddenly, he was on top and had fallen off with a flop onto the kitchen tiles, and then he began squealing for his mother.

Furble rescued him by the scruff, carried him back in, and, holding him down with a heavy paw, washed him 'til he squealed again.

"They'll all be out tomorrow," said Gran. "We won't be able to move for kittens. God help her. They'll drive her frantic."

David watched the kittens feeding. "They don't like each other much," he said. "They're clawing each other away from the nipples. They're trampling on each others' faces."

"Like each other?" said Gran. "You wait."

"Why do the kittens never do pooh?" said David.

"Well," said Gran, "if they did pooh all over the drawer, Furble would have to keep finding a new home for them. Cats are very clean and she just licks them on their rear ends and that keeps them clean until they are big enough to crawl by themselves to a place they choose to do pooh. That's why kittens are so easy to house-train. You just make sure they use the litter-tray when they are big enough – put them onto it, they'll soon learn."

Now the kittens were moving everywhere. They flew around the kitchen as erratically as autumn leaves, far better at moving than in knowing where they were going. Furble kept on picking them up, and returning them to the drawer, and they kept escaping again. She was frantic.

"She's like the old woman who lived in a shoe. She has so many children she doesn't know what to do. I'll put them in the old tea-chest to give her a bit of peace."

David eyed the towering sides of the tea-chest. "They'll never get out of that."

"I'll give them two days. Two days of peace for her. Two days of peace for us." Two days it was.

"Now's the time to find them homes," said Gran.

"But they're far too young to leave her."

"People who want kittens like to be in at the beginning. They like to come every week and see how their kitten's getting on. Here you are – magazines." She pushed a foot-high pile of magazines at David. "We're looking for pictures of kittens. Coloured pictures."

It was amazing how many pictures of kittens David found. Even in the *TV Times*.

"Five postcards," said Gran. "One each for the Post Office, the off-licence, the vet's, the corner-shop and the pet shop in town."

She stuck on each two pictures of ginger toms, one of a black kitten and one of a little white female. Then she took up a red felt-tip and wrote on each card: "VERY GOOD HOMES WANTED FOR ADORABLE KITTENS."

"All kittens are adorable," she said. "People just need reminding." Then she listed them.

"'ROMULUS AND REMUS'. TWIN GINGER TOMS.

'LUCKY'. A LUCKY BLACK TOM.

'SNOWDROP'. A PRETTY WHITE FEMALE."

"Why'd you give them names? People will want to give them their own names."

"I know they will," said Gran. "I once called a pair of tabby toms 'Starsky' and 'Hutch', but the people who took them called them 'Benson' and 'Hedges'. But it all helps to make the postcard more interesting. It'll be the female we'll have trouble finding a home for. Toms are easier to have 'done' and it costs less. But females make the best mousers and ratters, if people did but know it."

She gave David a pound coin. "Run down to the shops with the postcards. Don't give them the money until they've put the card in the window. Two weeks in each shop. That should do it."

And it did.

The phone rang two nights later. The family came round. Gran gave them coffee, and everybody sat round the kitchen, while the kittens wavered and wobbled round their feet.

"I'd like the little white one," said the little girl, cradling it to her cheek. Her mum looked worried. Very worried.

"I've always wanted a lucky black cat," she said at last.

"I've always fancied ginger toms," said the father.

"I think you're very wise," said Gran. "They'll be good company for each other. They'll have you in fits with their antics." She gave the father her most winning smile.

After that there wasn't much argument. The family departed asking if they could come back in a week, to see how their kittens were getting on.

"I like kittens to go in pairs," said Gran. "It's terrible what happens to single kittens. One day they've got their mum and all their brothers and sisters, and the next they're alone among strangers. That's when you've got to love them and cuddle them non-stop or..."

"Or what?"

"Or else they turn into very dull cats, who just don't like anybody. I've seen too many cats like that."

A couple came at the weekend. And chose the lucky black tom. Oddly, they liked the name "Lucky". But they didn't want the little white female, and nor, it seemed, did anybody else. David began to worry. What if they couldn't find a home? "Oh well," said Gran, "maybe we'll keep her for ourselves. Trouble is, that way, I could end up one of those ladies with twenty cats. It's very easily done, you know, if you're soft hearted and people know it. 'Snowdrop' could be having kittens of her own before long. Four months old when they start. Nature can be very cruel."

But it got forgotten in the fun of the riotous time. What Gran called "thunder-of-hooves-time". Kittens chasing each other everywhere, leaping on each other, crashing each other down, biting each other's necks until squeals become piteous. Lying in ambush, waggling their tiny bottoms, pouncing.

"They're practising killing each other," said Gran, swiftly rescuing Snowdrop, who was getting the worst of things.

Kittens could do so many things cats couldn't. Running sideways like crabs, running backwards, leaping two feet in the air from a standing four-footed start. Climbing Gran's curtains right to the top and then yowling from the curtain-rail because they couldn't get down again. Gran had to rescue them twenty times a day.

"Why don't grown-up cats do those things?" asked David.

"Expect they can, but they see no need for it," said Gran. "Just as well. I don't think my curtains could take another set of kittens."

"They purr like little bees. And spit like little fireworks."

"Yes, they're almost ready to go. If only for Furble's sake." The she-cat, thin as a rail with huge burning eyes, called and called to the kittens who no longer took a blind bit of notice. She ran among them like a frantic teacher who has lost control of her class.

"They've got her worn out, poor love. They're adolescents now."

They taught them to drink milk, upending them and plunging their noses into the saucer. The kittens, released, would sneeze milk all over, then lick their noses with their tiny tongues.

"They'll soon get a taste for milk," said Gran. "Look at that greedy beggar, with all four feet in the saucer."

Later David helped rub cat food on their faces. They soon got the idea of that, too. Kittens got trodden on; sat on by the vicar when he called. You could not move for kittens. Whenever you sat down, they climbed up your legs in the most excruciating way.

Furble began to attack the kittens, throwing them down and biting them, scrabbling them with her back legs. Finally, the kittens made a fort under Gran's chair, and kept driving off their mother with fierce blows, whenever she came near. But when she tried to lie down to rest, they leapt fiercely and bit her tail.

"Time to go," said Gran.

David sat in the silent kitchen. Lucky and Romulus and Remus (re-named Ginger and Red) had gone to their good homes. Gran had taken Furble to the vet's to be spayed.

"I always like a she-cat to have one litter – it makes them nicer natured. But no more – there's far too many kittens in the world already."

Snowdrop lay in a chair, asleep. She had spent a lot of the morning wandering around, looking for the others and mewing sadly. She looked very small and grown-up and lonely as she lay asleep. David picked her up and put her on his knee and stroked her gently with one finger. It would never do to have Snowdrop turn into a dull, boring cat.

Like a tiny bee, Snowdrop began to purr.

It would be all right: just a lot of loving to do.

A CAT AND LOVE

COLETTE

ONE DAY I noticed a poor thin cat being pushed to and fro by the crowd which pours each evening out of the Auteuil metro. In fact it was she who recognized me. "There you are at last," she said. "You are very late. Where is your home? Do not worry, I will follow you."

In the country she is flirtatious and promiscuous, delighting in her freedom to be truly catlike and not the human's "best friend". To me she is warm, faithful and sensitive – the opposite of all she is to her cat lovers.

In town, in the narrow walled garden of my Paris house, she played happily, sometimes full of energy, sometimes content to dream. She restrained her natural instincts haughtily rejecting would-be mates. There is the old striped conqueror, thin as a rake, bald in places but highly experienced. He is decisive, respected by his rivals, confident of success.

Then there is a young cat, stupid and self-satisfied, enjoying his own beauty – the beauty of the tiger. Finally, there is the farm cat who appears on the top of the wall as though awakened from a dream by an urgent mating call.

She gives all three a hard time using her paws without mercy to slap their faces when they push too hard. Then she rolls around in front of them but follows that exhibition with freezing contempt. She climbs onto a crumbling pillar from which she can pour scorn on her assailants. When she decides to rejoin her three slaves she does so with hauteur. She allows one of her admirers to kiss her nose but when this goes on too long she puts a stop to it with an imperious cry impossible to describe.

The three tomcats jump back in surprise. My cat, seeming to forget her lovers, goes back to grooming herself. Depressed by their long courtship, the male cats begin to fight amongst themselves to pass the time. My cat leaves them to it, renouncing her flirtatious games, pleased to rejoin the humans.

While I work, my cat lies beside me under the warmth of my reading lamp, silent, watchful, content – my she-cat, my friend.

VICKY

ROBERT WESTALL

VICKY WAS the runt of the litter; the runtiest runt I ever saw. Four pounds of skin and bone and thin black and white fur. We got her when she was three years old. We got her off a lady called Dawn Haddock, who had a large family, liberal feelings, not a lot of money and a hopeless weakness for strays. Finally, Dawn's husband put his foot down; one cat had to go. It was inevitable that it would be Vicky. Vicky was a born loser.

We were seized with an irresistible urge to love Vicky into success; we were young and green and full of hope then. We would love Vicky until she was like Wilhelmina. Wilhelmina was Vicky's sister; the same black back and white face and front; only three times the size, as sleek a beast as ever drew breath.

We might as well have saved our breath to cool our porridge. Vicky wasn't a runt by nurture; she was a runt by nature. She would turn up her nose at the best cat-food, and go and scrounge peas and carrots off the plates stacked for washing-up. Her favourite was bacon-rind put out in the yard for the birds, washed old and white by the rain. Turned her nose up at milk and drank from puddles.

Despairing, we fed her with loads of peas and old bacon-rind. Several times, she grew fat. But each time we sat back and said smugly, "I think Vicky's shaping up at last", she would be visited by a week of vomiting, until she returned to her usual scrawny shape. The vet could find nothing wrong. It was as if she just knew the shape she wanted to be; a feline anorexic.

She began tense; she remained tense. We couldn't understand this. The Haddocks were kindly, if impecunious. They would never have hurt a cat. Vicky had been born in their house and never known another home. Sister Wilhelmina was so relaxed she drooped on you like a fur rug.

33

Mind you, Vicky was *tense*, not nervous. She would go to anybody and sit in their lap. Tensely. It was like nursing a bundle of barbed wire. The more you stroked her, the tenser she got. She showed her pleasure by that extending and contracting of claws. The more you stroked, the more the claws bit through your trousers. She was the only cat I ever had that drew blood while in repose. She would plead to be on your knee, you would have compassion for about ten minutes, and then, when it got unbearable, you would shout, "For Christ's sake, Vicky", and shove her off. The only person who could stand her for long was our char, Phyllis, equally small, thin, wiry, and inured cheerfully to hard times. They were sisters under the skin, Vicky and Phyllis. As Vicky got older, her claws got worse. In the end she wasn't a lap-cat at all.

However many cats we had, she was always bottom of the peck order. There were never any quarrels where Vicky was concerned. She was bottom, and everybody knew it, including her.

Except where motherhood was concerned. We knew she'd never been neutered; there didn't seem enough *to* neuter; for three years she produced nothing. Then, just once, she reached the level of wellbeing that made her interesting to toms. We were terrified for her in pregnancy; she was like a bag walking about on sticks; we thought her pelvis would not allow an infant mouse through . . .

She had three large and healthy kittens without trouble. She was an excellent skeleton of a mother, with an appetite like a raging fire. By the time the kittens went to good homes, they were nearly as big as she was; they grew to be giants. After they had gone, she returned to eating peas.

But her great moment came when one of the younger she-cats got pregnant. A day before the birth, Mum moved into the traditional place, bottom drawer of the kitchen cupboard. Only, Vicky moved in with her. And in the moment of birth, it was Vicky who pounced on the kitten, tore off the birth-sack with a speed which made us think the kitten was being eaten alive, licked the kitten dry. When all was over, Mum and Vicky settled into a defensive O-shape, leg to leg, with the kittens between, all purring contentedly. After that, there was never a kitten born in the house who did not have Vicky for midwife; the younger females conceded her complete authority. I remember once, when we were going on holiday, taking Vicky, Mum and four-week kittens up to the kennels. We didn't bother with a basket. Mum and kittens on the back seat, comfortably feeding; Vicky superintending from the back windowsill. Until the car started. Then Mum

34

went into a total panic, flying around the car, trying to climb the windscreen or the driver's face. Kittens wailing and calling and crawling everywhere. Until Vicky took command, called the kittens to her and was soon lying on a contented heap. Including in the end, Mum for comfort.

The only unease Vicky ever showed was when the kittens made for her shrivelled dugs to feed. Then she would gently roll her body, to put herself out of the reach of sharp little teeth. But once the kittens were gone, back to her humble role she went.

Her other great performances were out of doors. We knew she had two other homes, because those who tried to entice her away came to the house and lectured us on our neglect of her meagre frame. Vicky's favourite victim was the milk-woman, a raw-boned foul-mouthed harridan of fifty-five who frequently started World War Three all up and down the street on the Saturday morning when she collected the milk money; bitter as gall over a penny-ha'penny on the account. Vicky would accompany the milk-cart all round the district, and the woman would talk to her all the way. She, above all, became convinced we were starving Vicky to death. She brought a saucer of her own, and left it permanently on our front doorstep. Into it she would daily broach a bottle of the dairy's gold-top milk, leaving the opened bottle for free beside it as a mute remonstrance to our cruelty. Our milk-bill was halved as a result, for months on end . . .

Somehow, Vicky was at her best with tough, scrawny, neglected women;

I think they empathised with her. She was very tough herself. Was run over by a motorbike and lay in the road all night with a broken pelvis, till our char found her and, greatly daring, in our absence on holiday, authorised treatment at the vet's. The vet said the pelvis would heal itself, without treatment, which it did. But her bowel clogged as a result of the accident, solid. The brilliant vet opened her up, the whole length of the main bowel, and cleaned it out by hand and sewed her up again. And she made a complete recovery.

But from passing time neither man nor cat can recover. The white hairs gathered on her black nose, her white fur went thinner and yellow, and her black fur thinner and brown. She followed the milk-cart only when the summer sun beckoned her; then she got no further than the front step, basking in the sunshine. And then it was just the back yard, then just the kitchen, and finally just her cardboard box and blanket by the stove. She did not suffer; only faded into a thin photograph of herself. But as she faded, her eyes grew enormous and enormously loving. No-one could enter the kitchen without a chirrup of greeting; and confined to her box, unable to dig her claws into anybody, she achieved at last the homage and affectionate petting she had always lacked.

I never forget the end; her usual jump for the windowsill, when her body failed her and she fell. And tried again, and fell again. And made it the third time with a desperate scramble. She was so *baffled* that her body had failed her.

Kidneys, of course. She was thirteen. We had always known she would never make old bones; but she didn't make young ones either. The creaking gate hung a long time.

We took her last journey to the vet. Her hind-legs had given out by that time; but as her body grew weaker, her soul grew, burning out of those enormous eyes turned on us. She knew, I think, that she was going; and she didn't want to go. She wasn't afraid; she just didn't want to leave us.

We stroked her as the needle went in. For a second, as she felt the last enemy coming through her veins she was intensely alive again; all senses turned to track and fight the foe.

And then she sighed, and was only a scrap of bone and fur. I was surprised there was so little left, when the soul had gone. But she'd always been two-thirds spirit, anyway.

THE LEVERET

GILBERT WHITE (18TH CENTURY)

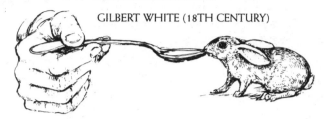

MY FRIEND had a little helpless leveret brought to him, which the servants fed with milk in a spoon, and about the same time his cat kittened and the young were dispatched and buried. The hare was soon lost, and supposed to be gone the way of most foundlings, to be killed by some dog or cat. However, in about a fortnight, as the master was sitting in his garden in the dusk of an evening, he observed his cat, with tail erect, trotting towards him, and calling with little short inward notes of complacency, such as they use towards their kittens, and something gambolling after, which proved to be the leveret that the cat had supported with her milk, and continued to support with great affection.

This strange affection probably was occasioned by those tender maternal feelings, which the loss of her kittens had awakened in her breast; and by the complacency and ease she derived to herself from the procuring her teats to be drawn, which were too much distended with milk, till, from habit, she became as much delighted with this foundling, as if it had been her real offspring.

THE LEGACY

ANDREW LANG

AN OLD lady cat felt that she was dying before her kittens were weaned. She could hardly walk, but she disappeared one morning carrying a kitten, and came back without it. Next day, quite exhausted, she did this with her other two kittens, and then died. She had carried each kitten to a separate cat, each of which was nourishing a family, and accepted the new fosterling. Can anything be wiser or more touching? This poor old cat had memory, reflection, reason. Though wordless, she was as much a thinking creature as any man who makes his last will and testament.

Other cats came, with kind enquiries, to visit a puss whose leg had been hurt in a rabbit trap. One of them, having paid her visit, went out, caught a rabbit, and brought it back to the sufferer. What sportsman could do more?

Some cats are snobs, though not so many cats as dogs share this human infirmity. A lady had two cats; one was a drawing-room cat, the other a common kitchen cat. Both, simultaneously, had families. The drawing-room cat carried her kittens downstairs to be nursed by the common kitchen cat, but every day she visited the nursery several times. She was not quite heartless, but she had never read Jean-Jacques Rousseau, on the nursing of children, and she was very aristocratic.

From THE KITTEN
AND THE FALLING LEAVES

WILLIAM WORDSWORTH

See the kitten on the wall
Sporting with the leaves that fall,
Withered leaves – one – two – and three –
From the lofty elder tree!

– But the kitten, how she starts,
Crouches, stretches, paws and darts!
First at one, and then its fellow
Just as light and just as yellow;
There are many now – now one –
Now they stop and there are none.
What intenseness of desire
In her upward eyes of fire!
With a tiger-leap half way
Now she meets the coming prey,
Lets it go as fast, and then
Has it in her power again:
How she works with three or four,
Like an Indian conjurer,
Quick as he in feats of art,
Far beyond in joy of heart . . .

LITTLE CAT LOST

ROBERT WESTALL

I T WAS a monumental stupidity, from the beginning. We were on
holiday, two hundred miles from home. But we were short of one cat,
and the notice,
"GOOD HOMES WANTED FOR KITTENS"
is always seductive. We had no cat basket with us, the car was already
chock-a-block with antiques, and becoming a baking oven, in the midst of
the great heatwave of 1984 but,
"GOOD HOMES WANTED FOR KITTENS".

We found the house; a charming rambling farmhouse. The owner was
sitting on the back doorstep in jeans and open-necked shirt, a relaxed man
of fifty who had turned from hi-tech to country living. Two kittens were in
the garden with their mother, who was relaxing in the sun, her kitten-
rearing duties done. Both kittens were ready to leave home; perfect little
miniature cats who had just gained the grace of composure; very proper
little miniatures. She came straight to us and jumped into my arms.

"That's the friendly one," the owner said. "But she's already spoken for."

The other had retreated delicately into the sanctuary of a bottomless
plastic watering-can lying on its side; it was that sort of back garden.
There, quite composed in her castle, she received us with condescension.
"She's in a friendly mood this morning, thank God," said the owner.
"Otherwise she'd get into the bushes and we'd never catch her."

That is how I remember her; in her primal paradise, in her strong castle,
with her clumps of refuge-bushes around her, and her mother and sister
nearby in the sunny garden. The paradise we'd come to take her away from
forever. Ah well, she'd soon settle down with Welly and Vanessa and
Mirabelle . . .

We had a long cultured talk about this and that, and then the owner produced a cardboard box and popped her in, and overleafed the flaps, the way antique-dealers do. We left a little airhole, it was so hot.

That was the first mistake; she had her head out of the box before we'd finished saying goodbye to the owner, and once she'd got the trick of it, she could crack the box in three seconds. We wound up the car windows to a two-inch gap at the top.

As we drove away waving, she leapt onto my shoulder and dived through the two-inch gap. I just managed to haul her back by the hind-legs; it did not improve her confidence in me.

We wound up the windows to half-an-inch; the car immediately became a sweatbox. Snowflake, as we had provisionally called her, since she was nearly all white, with ginger and black along the back, mountaineered grandly over the antique clocks in the back, my shoulders, my wife's shoulders; we nearly ran into the back of a parked car in the main street of Beaminster. Then she settled down under the driver's seat, in horrible proximity to the brake-pedal . . .

But she went quiet. Or asphyxiated. Every ten miles, I felt under the seat to make sure she was still breathing. We had to park at Shaftesbury for toilets; crept away leaving the windows that half inch down, thinking of all the warnings the RSPCA had ever issued. She was still alive when we got back; just moribund, we thought.

Just south of Warminster my wife became convinced she was dying for lack of air. We pulled off at a picnic place, a huge piece of arid grass. We laid her out on the grass and bent over her anxiously.

She made a fast beeline for the nearest hedge. From near-corpse to Olympic sprinter in one-tenth of a second. I dived for her in a rugby-tackle as she reached the edge of the hedge; my hand touched her tail, but I couldn't clench my fist quick enough. She vanished into the hedge, leaving me with two grazed elbows and two bruised knees. We peered into the darkness, and saw her little white face peering warily out. Optimistically we called and twitched fingers. She did not budge. We suddenly realised there was no reason why she should. We had kidnapped her, imprisoned her, half-roasted her, joggled her up and down, subjected her to hideous new noises. And now she was quiet, hidden, cool, and thought she knew exactly where she was. She probably thought this hedge led straight back to her own garden. She probably thought all her problems were over.

We tried a saucer of half-warm milk (all the milk was half-warm by that time) and some of the Kit-e-Kat we'd bought for her in Shaftesbury. She

41

proved unsusceptible to such blatant bribery by kidnappers.

Well, if the mountain would not come to Mohammed, Mohammed must go to the mountain. I would go into the hedge after her; my wife would wait in the field behind to cut off her retreat.

It was only then that I realised what kind of hedge it was. Not so much a hawthorn hedge as a small hawthorn forest, ten yards thick and fifty long. Where there wasn't hawthorn there were brambles, and where there weren't brambles there were stinging-nettles. Slowly and painfully, I started to excavate my first motorway through. I was nearly disembowelled in the first ten seconds. To the works of God had been added the works of man. In the stinging-nettles, a broken bottle. A rusty open tin. A crushed colander. There was no litter-bin at the lay-by. The hedge was the litter-bin. And half-way through, a barbed wire fence . . .

I pushed Motorway One right through. Snowflake simply waited till the last moment, then retreated five yards further. Motorway Two. Motorway Three. Always, she watched me, with unwavering interest. I called to her, waved the plate of drying-out Kit-e-Kat, the saucer of now cheeselike milk. She would advance slowly towards me, like a tiger perfectly at home in her jungle. Those were the brief moments of tranquil beauty, with me lying at cat's-eye level, watching my tiger in miniature moving towards me. She even came as far as sniffing my outstretched crucified fingers. But before my fingers could close on her neck, she was gone.

After three hours, I gave up. I had no tricks left to try. I knew I could never catch her. And from being a two o'clock lunch-stop, it was now five. And we were still 150 miles from home.

My wife began to cry. I asked her what the hell she was crying about. My wife said we would have to leave her. Forever. I said no way; there had to be a solution. If man could put travellers onto the moon . . . Then the wave of weariness hit me. I could hardly put one foot in front of another. My beach-shirt was splattered with blood from my wounds. I was shaking all over and couldn't think straight. I had nothing left to give. Nothing at all. I just could not believe there wasn't a solution. But think as I might, there wasn't. She had beaten me, and signed her own death-warrant. Her fortress would no longer be a strong castle once night fell, and the cold came, and the hunger, and the fox and the weasel, sniffing her out. Not a house in sight. Nothing but busy roads . . .

We gave her the last things we could give her. A fresh saucer of milk, and the rest of the Kit-e-Kat on the old picnic-plate. Then we left her to her fate; six weeks old.

I could not map-read any more: we kept getting lost in suburbs and going round in circles. My wife could hardly drive. We had two near-misses in ten miles. I just could not believe we had just done the wickedest thing in our lives; the feelings of guilt were a blizzard. My wife kept crying and having to pull off the road.

We reached Leominster eventually, and had a wretched cup of tea and a sandwich in a cafe. I was absurdly grateful to the proprietress for deigning to serve two such wicked people; for accepting us back into the human race, even if she didn't know what we'd done. My wife, ever-hopeful, tried to contact the RSPCA. She found the nearest office was Gloucester, sixty miles away. They said they would do what they could . . . well, they would have to say that, wouldn't they?

And so we came home, all the benefits of a fortnight's holiday totally undone. And with the memory of Snowflake, waiting, trusting, as darkness fell, and the fox, and starvation, and the weasel. I preached a moving sermon on her, at our prayer-group. How she had thought she knew best; thought herself safe when the most frightful end was approaching. How she did not know we were going away, and with us all hope of warmth and food and comfort. How like the human condition . . . vis-à-vis God. The audience was visibly moved.

The RSPCA rang us, two days later. They had been to check. A passer-by had told them that Snowflake wandered out friendly and charming, to the first person who passed on the Monday morning. Made it clear she was lost and bereft. Been taken to the cottage of an old lady who already had five other cats. The old lady said she was now nicely settled in; the RSPCA weren't going to take her away again, were they? What did we want them to do?

We left her with her new-found old lady. We felt we had no right to do anything else.

THE ENEMIES OF CATS

THE CATS OF ULTHAR

H.P. LOVECRAFT

I T IS said that in Ulthar, which lies beyond the river Skai, no man may
kill a cat; and this I can verily believe as I gaze upon him who sitteth
purring before the fire. For the cat is cryptic, and close to strange things
which men cannot see. He is the soul of antique Aegyptus, and bearer of
tales from forgotten cities in Meroe and Ophir. He is the kin of the jungle's
lords and heir to the secrets of hoary and sinister Africa. The Sphinx is his
cousin, and he speaks her language; but he is more ancient than the Sphinx,
and remembers that which she hath forgotten.

In Ulthar, before ever the burgesses forbade the killing of cats, there
dwelt an old cotter and his wife who delighted to trap and slay cats of their
neighbours. Why they did this I do not know; save that many hate the voice
of the cat in the night, and take it ill that cats should run stealthily about

yards and gardens at twilight. But whatever the reason, this old man and woman took pleasure in trapping and slaying every cat which came near to their hovel; and from some of the sounds heard after dark, many villagers fancied that the manner of slaying was exceedingly peculiar.

But the villagers did not discuss such things with the old man and his wife; because of the habitual expression on the withered faces of the two, and because their cottage was so small and so darkly hidden under spreading oaks and at the back of a neglected yard. In truth, much as the owners of cats hated these old folk, they feared them more; and instead of berating them as brutal assassins, merely took care that no cherished pet or mouser should stray towards the remote hovel under the dark trees. When through some unavoidable oversight a cat was missed, and sounds were heard after dark, the loser would lament impotently; or console himself by thanking Fate that it was not one of his children who had thus vanished. For the people of Ulthar were simple, and knew not whence it is all cats first came.

One day a caravan of strange wanderers from the South entered the narrow cobbled streets of Ulthar. Dark wanderers they were, and unlike the other roving folk who passed through the village twice every year. In the market-place they told fortunes for silver, and bought gay beads from the merchants. What was the land of these wanderers none could tell; but it was seen that they were given to strange prayers and that they had painted on the sides of their wagons strange figures with human bodies and the heads of cats, hawks, rams and lions. And the leader of the caravan wore a head-dress with two horns and a curious disc between the horns.

There was in this singular caravan a little boy with no father or mother, but only a tiny black kitten to cherish. The plague had not been kind to him, yet had left him this small furry thing to mitigate his sorrow; and when one is very young, one can find great relief in the lively antics of a black kitten. So the boy whom the dark people called Menes smiled more often than he wept as he sat playing with his graceful kitten on the steps of an oddly painted wagon.

On the third morning of the wanderers' stay in Ulthar, Menes could not find his kitten; and as he sobbed aloud in the market-place certain villagers told him of the old man and his wife, and of sounds heard in the night. And when he heard these things his sobbing gave way to meditation, and finally prayer. He stretched out his arms towards the sun and prayed in a tongue no villager could understand; though indeed the villagers did not try very hard to understand, since their attention was mostly taken up by the sky and the odd shapes the clouds were assuming. It was very peculiar, but as the little boy uttered his petition there seemed to form overhead the shadowy, nebulous figures of exotic things; of hybrid creatures crowned with horn-flanked discs. Nature is full of such illusions to impress the imaginative.

That night the wanderers left Ulthar, and were never seen again. And the householders were troubled when they noticed that in all the village there was not a cat to be found. From each hearth the familiar cat had vanished; cats large and small, black, grey, striped, yellow and white. Old Kranon, the burgomaster, swore that the dark folks had taken the cats away in revenge for the killing of Menes' kitten; and cursed the caravan and the little boy. But Nith, the lean notary, declared that the old cotter and his wife were more likely persons to suspect; for their hatred of cats was notorious and increasingly bold.

Still, no one durst complain to the sinister couple; even when little Atal, the innkeeper's son, vowed that he had at twilight seen all the cats of Ulthar in that accursed yard under the trees, pacing very slowly and solemnly in a circle around the cottage, two abreast, as if in performance of some unheard-of rite of beasts. The villagers did not know how much to believe from so small a boy; and though they feared that the evil pair had charmed the cats to their death, they preferred not to chide the old cotter till they met him outside his dark and repellent yard.

So Ulthar went to sleep in vain anger; and when the people awakened at dawn — behold! every cat was back at his accustomed hearth! Large and small, black, grey, striped, yellow and white, none was missing. Very sleek and fat did the cats appear, and sonorous with purring content. The citizens talked with one another of the affair, and marvelled not a little. Old Kranon again insisted that it was the dark folk who had taken them, since cats did not return alive from the cottage of the ancient man and his wife. But all agreed on one thing; that the refusal of the cats to eat their portions of meat or to drink their saucers of milk was exceedingly curious, and for two whole days the sleek, lazy cats of Ulthar would touch no food, but only doze by the fire or in the sun.

It was fully a week before the villagers noticed that no lights were appearing at dusk in the windows of the cottage under the trees. Then the lean Nith remarked that no one had seen the old man or his wife since the night the cats were away. In another week the burgomaster decided to overcome his fears and call at the strangely silent dwelling as a matter of duty, though in doing so he was careful to take with him Shang the blacksmith and Thul the cutter of stone as witnesses. And when they had broken down the frail door they found only this: two cleanly picked human skeletons on the earthen floor, and a number of singular beetles crawling in the shadowy corners.

There was subsequently much talk among the burgesses of Ulthar. Zath, the coroner, disputed at length with Nith, the lean notary; and Kranon and Shang and Thul were overwhelmed with questions. Even little Atal, the innkeeper's son, was closely questioned and given a sweetmeat as reward. They talked of the old cotter and his wife, of the caravan of dark wanderers, of small Menes and his black kitten, of the prayer of Menes and of the sky during that prayer, of the doing of the cats on the night the caravan left, and of what was later found in the cottage under the dark trees in the repellent yard.

And in the end the burgesses passed that remarkable law which is told of by traders in Hatheg and discussed by travellers in Nir; namely, that in Ulthar no man may kill a cat.

CAT ENEMIES

DAVID GREENE

WHEN NOT at the keyboard, Brahms' favourite form of relaxation seems to have been sitting at an open window and attempting, usually with success, to kill neighbouring cats with a bow and arrow . . .

During our campaign, an aide to Napoleon was startled by the emperor calling loudly for assistance. Opening the door, he discovered his master half naked, sweating with fear and lunging wildly with his sword at a small kitten.

Eisenhower's staff had orders to shoot any cats seen in the grounds of his Gettysburg home.

THE CAT AND FRIENDSHIP

JUBILATE AGNO

CHRISTOPHER SMART (18TH CENTURY)

For I will consider my Cat Jeoffrey.

For he is the servant of the Living God, duly and daily serving him.

For at the first glance of the glory of God in the East, he worships in his way.

For this is done by wreathing his body seven times round with elegant quickness.

For then he leaps up to catch the musk, which is the blessing of God upon his prayer.

For he rolls upon the prank to work it in.

For having done duty and received blessing he begins to consider himself.

For this he performs in ten degrees.

For first he looks upon his forepaws, to see if they are clean.

For secondly he kicks up behind to clear away there.

For thirdly he works it upon stretch with the forepaws extended.

For fourthly he sharpens his paws by wood.

For fifthly he washes himself.

For sixthly he rolls upon wash.

For seventhly he fleas himself, that he may not be interrupted upon the beat.

For eighthly he rubs himself against a post.

For ninthly he looks up for his instructions.

For tenthly he goes in quest of food.

For having considered God and himself he will consider his neighbour.
For if he meets another cat he will kiss her in kindness.
For when he takes his prey he plays with it to give it chance.
For one mouse in seven escapes by his dallying.
For when his day's work is done his business more properly begins.
For he keeps the Lord's watch in the night against the adversary.
For he counteracts the powers of darkness by his electrical skin and
    glaring eyes.
For he counteracts the Devil, who is death, by brisking about the life.
For in his morning orisons he loves the sun and the sun loves him.
For he is of the tribe of Tiger.
For the Cherub Cat is a term of the Angel Tiger.

SUMMER IN CAMBRIDGE

ROBERT WESTALL

I T SEEMED such a lovely idea; renting a house in Cambridge for the
summer. From a college. Sleep six. We could even invite friends for the
weekend. Be gracious.

I should've been warned by my reception at the college. Shunted from
porter to post, a thing of low degree. Warned to keep off the grass, before I
had gone two paces, by a hidden observer. I had a feeling of censorious eyes
everywhere, waiting for me to steal a dustbin, of which there were many,
placed very prominently.

I had to prove to the person in charge who I was. Their letter of
acceptance wasn't enough. Only a driving licence would do. I had to pay the
full rent before I got the keys. The keys were explained to me as if I were a
cretin. A long string of do's and don'ts followed, as her bun, which couldn't
have been stretched tighter round her head, waggled censoriously; I was
found guilty and condemned for all the sins of the previous tenants. Then
released to stagger away.

They hadn't bothered to explain in their advertisement that the house, so
very conveniently placed for the town centre was on the main arterial road
south. That it shook, every time a juggernaut thundered past, which was
about every two minutes. Day and night. They hadn't explained the narrow
darkness of the house; the difficulty of getting the painted-up windows
open, in the roasting weather. The narrow discomfort of the beds and
chairs, fit only for the slim, well-muscled backsides of future gym-teachers.
The payphone in the hall, surrounded by a desperate web of scribbled Biro
graffiti. The bare greyness of the walls, mottled with a glitter of pink and
blue, where the students had tried to humanise the place by sticking posters
to the wall with Blu-Tack and Buddies. The narrow garden; a billiard-table
of grass mown once a week by the college gardener, and three dustbins.

We sat with our luggage round us; I doubt Giant Despair could've done worse in Doubting Castle.

And then, as if by magic, three black furry faces appeared at the French windows. Three pink triangles of mouth, demanding to be fed.

They were, of course. Twice a day. At first with scraps of steak-and-kidney pie, but later with tinned cat-food. They had such a grave politeness; they were so punctual, like three rising young dons coming back from lectures into hall for dinner. So infinitely belonging. And the only welcoming thing in the whole wretched place.

But the odd thing was, they would never come into the house. No matter how tempting the food, no matter how small a distance inside the open French window, they never crossed the threshold; never laid one paw over it. Outside, they ate heartily, allowed themselves to be stroked in moderation as they ate. A mother and two grown kittens, we thought, one kitten stocky and solid, the other more angular and academic, with a hint of Siamese father.

They didn't linger, once they'd finished eating. Oh, it was exasperating! We were supposed to be *good* with cats. In all the time we were there, we didn't make a dent in their wariness.

I got no warmer a welcome when I finally returned the keys to the College Person. Her manner implied that if I hadn't absconded with the wretched furniture it was owing to lack of wit or initiative.

I had to have one last try to crack that stony face; to have it admit that I, and she, were both human beings; belonged to the same species.

"We enjoyed the company of your three cats," I said.

Her face, if anything, grew harder. If it was rock before, it was the frozen rock of Ultima Thule now.

"Are those *creatures* still there?" she intoned, like a judge wearing a black cap. "I thought they were dealt with. I shall speak to Greaves, and they will be dealt with straight away." I had no illusion about what she meant. I had just condemned three friends to death.

I looked at that suddenly hateful face, and knew there was no appeal. No good saying they must have been the only bright spot that her students had found in that house; that they were obviously much-loved rogues; that they were life itself. It's no good pleading life to the face of Death. Had she ever loved anything enough, not to tidy it away into death? Had there ever, under that stony academic exterior, been a spark of life?

If there had been, it had departed long since. I grabbed wildly in my mind for succour for my black friends. The police, the RSPCA, the UN . . .

Nothing. Nothing except to exclude her from the human race, from the loyalty that man owes as a species. To lie.

"Oh," I said. "They aren't strays. They've got collars..." Can a rock show alarm? I pressed on. "They belong to a man about four doors away. Big, very unpleasant bloke. He told us off for feeding them. Came to the door to complain. Very nasty. Couldn't get rid of him for hours. Thought he was going to get violent. Thought it might get to be a police matter."

Yes, real doubt is showing now. This she understands; the peasants have revolted against her before, with their vile gestures and viler language, their inexplicable rage at being trampled under her feet. She casts me a glance, almost of anguish. Am I telling her the truth?

I leave, at least satisfied she knows I hate her.

I thought about my three friends all the long journey home. My main comfort was not my cheap lies, but their own steadfast discipline never to enter the house; if ever the door is shut on them, their fate is sealed; no matter how they run and dodge and claw.

But no doubt, outside, they will lead Greaves his usual merry dance.

SIR HENRY WYATT

THOMAS SCOTT OF EGRESTON ESQ (16TH CENTURY)

. . . hee was imprisoned often, once in a cold and narrow tower, where he had neither bed to lie on, nor cloaths sufficient to warme him, nor meate for his mouth: he had starved there, had not God (who sent a crowe to feed his Prophet) sent a cat both to feede and warme him: a cat came one day down into the Dungeon unto him: and as it were offered herself unto him, hee was glad of her, laide her on his bosome to warme him, and by making much of her, won her love; after this, shee would come every day unto him, divers times and when shee could gett one, bring him a pigeon: hee complained to his keeper of his cold and short fare. The answer was hee (the keeper) durst not better itt: but said Sir Henry, if I can provide any, will you promise to dress (cook) it for me? I may well enough, said the keeper and dressed for him from time to time such pigeons as the cat provided for him. Sir Henry Wyatt in his prosperity, for this, would ever make much of a cat, as other men will of their spaniels or hounds: and perhaps you shall not find his picture anywhere but (like Sir Christopher Hatton with his dog) with a cat beside him.

THE LADY WHO NEEDED A CAT

MONCRIF

Translated by
REGINALD BRETNOR

SOMETIMES a fondness for cats is carried to the extreme. This past autumn, in a little village called Passy, situated on the Evreux route, a lady who came from Paris with a great retinue, arrived very late at a very mediocre hostelry: her first care before descending from her carriage was to demand if there was a cat in the house: they told her there was not: but they promised her marvels in all other respects: she replied that there had to be a cat for her, and that without one she would not be able to stay: they at once went to wake the whole village, and they finally brought her the female cat of the curé's: as soon as she had taken her up in her arms, the lady entered the hostelry and believed herself in the Palace of Psyche. She vowed that whenever she passed the night in an apartment where there was no cat at all, she was seized by insupportable vapours. Her health suffered badly whenever she was away: she was reduced to borrowing one at each stop she made, and whenever she could find none, she passed the night in the open.

53

PANGUR BÁN

*Written by a student of the monastery of Carinthia on a copy of
St Paul's Epistles, in the eighth century*

Translated from the Gaelic by
ROBIN FLOWER

I and Pangur Bán my cat,
'Tis a like task we are at;
Hunting mice is his delight,
Hunting words I sit all night.

Better far than praise of men
'Tis to sit with book and pen;
Pangur bears me no ill-will,
He too plies his simple skill.

'Tis a merry thing to see
At our tasks how glad are we,
When at home we sit and find
Entertainment to our mind.

Oftentimes a mouse will stray
In the hero Pangur's way;
Oftentimes my keen thought set
Takes a meaning in its net.

'Gainst the wall he sets his eye
Full and fierce and sharp and sly;
'Gainst the wall of knowledge I
All my little wisdom try.

When a mouse darts from its den,
O how glad is Pangur then!
O what gladness do I prove
When I solve the doubts I love!

So in peace our tasks we ply,
Pangur Bán, my cat, and I;
In our arts we find our bliss,
I have mine and he has his.

Practice every day has made
Pangur perfect in his trade;
I get wisdom day and night
Turning darkness into light.

TO MRS REYNOLDS' CAT

JOHN KEATS

Cat! who hast pass'd thy grand climacteric,
How many mice and rats hast in thy days
Destroy'd? How many tit bits stolen? Gaze
With those bright languid segments green, and prick
Those velvet ears – but pr'y thee do not stick
Thy latent talons in me – and upraise
Thy gentle mew – and tell me all thy frays,
Of fish and mice, and rats and tender chick.
Nay, look not down, nor lick thy dainty wrists –
For all thy wheezy asthma – and for all
Thy tail's tip is nick'd off – and though the fists
Of many a maid have given thee many a maul,
Still is that fur as soft, as when the lists
In youth thou enter'dest on glass bottled wall.

THE WOMAN'S FRIEND

AFRICAN TRADITIONAL

THE FOLLOWING tale is told among certain African tribes. The cat, conscious of his dignity and importance, resolved only to be friendly to the strongest and most powerful of living creatures. Having seen a hare put to flight by a jackal, he became friendly with the latter, only to scorn it when he saw it frightened by a leopard. His new friend, the leopard, was driven away by a lion, the lion frightened by a charging elephant, and the elephant killed and eaten by a man. Satisfied that he had at last, found "the lord of creation" whom no other creature could withstand, the cat transferred his friendship to the man. For many moons they hunted together, then one day the man returned to his home, and entered, leaving the cat waiting for him outside in the sun. Suddenly a loud shrill sound of anger rose in the hut, and the "lord of creation" rushed out, pale and trembling, followed by a volley of pots and pans. Curious to see the powerful being who could put to ignominious flight the conqueror of all other creatures, the cat walked into the hut and saw — a woman. Since that time, he has always remained her friend.

AT THE ZOO

MARK TWAIN

IN THE great Zoological Gardens (of Marseilles) we found specimens of all the animals the world produces, I think . . . The boon companion of the colossal elephant was a common cat! This cat had a fashion of climbing up the elephant's hind legs, and roosting on his back. She would sit up there, with her paws curved under her breast, and sleep in the sun half the afternoon. It used to annoy the elephant at first and he would reach up and take her down, but she would go aft and climb up again. She persisted until she finally conquered the elephant's prejudices, and now they are inseparable friends. The cat plays about her comrade's forefeet or his trunk often, until dogs approach, and then she goes aloft out of danger. The elephant has annihilated several dogs lately, that pressed his companion too closely.

TO A CAT

ALGERNON CHARLES SWINBURNE

Stately, kindly, lordly friend,
　　Condescend
Here to sit by me, and turn
Glorious eyes that smile and burn,
Golden eyes, love's lustrous meed,
On the golden page I read.

All your wondrous wealth of hair,
　　Dark and fair,
Silken-shaggy, soft and bright
As the clouds and beams of night,
Pays my reverent hand's caress
Back with friendlier gentleness.

Dogs may fawn on all and some
　　As they come;
You, a friend of loftier mind,
Answer friends alone in kind,
Just your foot upon my hand
Softly bids it understand.

THE CAT AND DOMESTIC LIFE

MILK FOR THE CAT

HAROLD MONRO

When the tea is brought at five o'clock,
And all the neat curtains are drawn with care,
The little black cat with bright green eyes
Is suddenly purring there.
At first she pretends, having nothing to do,
She has come in merely to blink by the grate,
But though tea may be late
Or the milk may be sour,
She is never late.
The white saucer like some full moon descends
At last from the cloud of the table above;
She sighs and dreams and thrills and glows,
Transfigured with love.
She nestles over the shining rim,
Buries her chin in the creamy sea;
Her tail hangs loose; each drowsy paw
Is doubled under each bending knee.
A long dim ecstasy holds her life;
Her world is an infinite shapeless white,
Till her tongue has curled the last holy drop
Then she sinks back into the night,
Draws and dips her body to heap
Her sleepy nerves in the great arm-chair,
Lies defeated and buried deep
Three or four hours unconscious there.

SECRET LIVES

ROBERT WESTALL

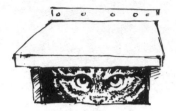

THANKS TO the cat-flap, there was a considerable secret life in our kitchen. But the kitchen is twenty yards from the lounge round a U-turn, and for a long time it remained secret.

The kitchen was an ideal place for a cat parliament. For one thing, the cats were able, via sink-unit and work-surface, mantelpiece and Welsh dressers, to circumnavigate it at waist-height without ever touching the floor, which the cats much preferred. The cold floor of red quarry-tiles was used only for playing Biro-football, with lots of satisfying rebounds off chair and table legs. We never had to look for a Biro; they were always under the convector-heater.

Also on the floor was the litter tray, always lined with a complete copy of *The Times*. In changing it, I often came across for the first time, absolutely indispensable articles; as a result, I have one valuable but extremely smelly file. The cats abandoned the tray for the summer, in April. The final, clean, copy, usually April 5th, lay all summer, when the tray was used for sleep by the current litter of kittens.

The other valued things at floor-level were the old fitted cupboards. Welly habitually slept there, on the bottom shelf, carving a neat furry cat-shaped nest among piles of disused mugs and saucers, in preference to the cat-baskets. Welly was a specialist in difficult and dangerous sleep. She would curl up on the ledge around the sink-unit, packing her large bulk into the corner where the weights of the pressure-cooker were kept, and holding her station with one ear cocked and one eye half-open, even while the washing up was being done, or a pressure-cooker de-pressurised about three inches from her nose. Occasionally, she got very wet, but did not seem to mind. She was always a sink-cat. As a kitten she spent hours contemplating a

60

dripping tap, with the odd dab of the paw; consequently she was always damp behind her left ear.

She was the supreme cupboard-cat too. When she was pregnant we got the bottom drawer cleared for her as usual. But on the morning when Phyllis noticed she had regained her sylph-like figure, there was no sign of kittens in the drawer. After a frantic search, we found them on the open and unguarded top shelf of the laundry cupboard, eight feet from the ground. Nature is not always wonderful.

Welly was a great one for being *contained*. The moment any cardboard box, however small, was left in the kitchen, she was crammed in it with that look of satisfaction and infinite superiority that only cats achieve. Once ensconced, she would attack the corners with her claws, until the walls of the box collapsed and she would have to seek a new home.

On the floor, too, was Mirabelle's refuge – under the kitchen cupboard. We got Mirabelle when she was a huge fat three-year-old tabby, of very placid disposition. Vanessa, a tortoiseshell cat less than half her size, but utterly queen of the pack, spent a month putting in vicious charges at her, which would certainly have cost Mirabelle her eyes, had not Mirabelle always sat by the kitchen cupboard, and economically slid beneath it at the last moment, leaving Vanessa to crash her head ten times a day into the bottom drawer. After a month, in which we sincerely feared Vanessa might suffer serious brain-damage, she finally despaired of ever thrusting an attack home, and there was an uneasy peace. A fine case of a cat out-stubborning a cat.

Above waist-height, there were succeeding levels of high cupboards, from which the she-cats could look down and sneer at each other and ourselves. The more agile cats could also circumnavigate the kitchen at ceiling-level; it took some of our guests a lot of courage to continue drinking their tea while cats passed overhead at ten feet altitude. There were no actual collisions, though several near-misses in mid-air; and a sleeping cat would occasionally fall from a great height, landing in the washing-up in the sink with a great clatter and splash, and slinking away utterly ashamed at such uncatlike lack of agility.

But this was their open life. For half the day, and all the evening till supper-drinks, they had the kitchen to themselves. And they would entertain. Especially in the winter, they had much to offer visitors. They were chronically overfed, and had half-empty saucers of food and drink which they allowed visitors to consume, at the expense of having their ears thoroughly sniffed while eating. And there was the electric stove, with the oven left on "low" from our forgetfulness or charity when nights were particularly cold. I have seen five cats stretched out on the stove-top, a tangled heap like the Raft of Medusa, with the fifth clinging on for dear life by a claw hooked through the radiant-ring. There was the odd case of singed fur from feline mistakes made during the working day, but only from Bella who was the stupidest. Otherwise the frequent and awful smell of burning was just from discarded fur left behind after grooming.

The visitors were all toms, three whole and one neutered; all past fathers of the she-cat's kittens. That was the way cats joined the club. It made the kitchen, I suppose into a feline cross between a cheerful 19th century French brothel, of the sort Toulouse-Lautrec lived in, and a home for battered wives. Not all the toms were equally popular. Felix, the enormous ginger neuter from next door, father of Welly's three, the week before his chances were ruined forever, was, in a sense, the brothel-keeper. He didn't come to eat; and obviously not to mate. He came simply because they were on what he considered his premises. He would inspect; he would dish out a moderate amount of punishment in the way of belted ears, indiscriminately, just to keep them from getting above themselves. All the shes were scared of him, except Sheba, who could sidestep him and sell him a dummy, wrong-foot him as cunningly as John McEnroe. Try as he might, he could never lay a paw on her, indoors or out. She was his constant companion, watching him with her cold, clever, half-Siamese eyes, constantly computing space and distance and angle of attack, the way only a clever cat can. Always outwitted, he never quite despaired of landing her one. So from her being his toy, he became hers. She treated him with the elegant contempt with

which a bullfighter treats a bull, even sitting a yard from him, towards the end, with her back completely turned, tempting his flagging spirits. She was the only cat that ever made a fool of him, for otherwise he was a dour and courageous fighter, of whom the full toms were terrified. He fought more savagely for his territory than they fought for mates, in the mating season, when our females came on heat.

He was middle-aged, utterly dignified in his slow thoughtful tread, never had reason for that sudden nervous look behind that most cats give. He would greet me; in moderation. Gruffly, and only for about thirty seconds, after which, if I persisted, he would have a dab at me, and mean it. Yet he never failed to greet me, dropping from his hole in the hedge, on top of the low wall, when I returned home. Had he been human, he would doubtless have called me "Westall" in that abrupt Cambridge way. He reminded me of Evelyn Waugh in his later years, gruff and rude, and yet with traditional courtesies, at bay in his stately home from the vulgar herd. Sheba, of course, inhabited his hole in the hedge at every opportunity.

Black Tom, on the other hand, was well-liked by our she-cats, if well-sniffed. If Felix was Evelyn Waugh, Black Tom was Charles Bronson. He was old, and his back was brown; his ears were rags, and the top of his head was crisscrossed with old scars and one or two new and open ones. Broad in the head and shoulders, with that slender macho swagger of lean muscular hips. He only came into the kitchen when the weather was truly dreadful, sleet or ice or rain, when he had been driven out of his summer retreat. My wife used to chase him out, if he came too early while we were still finishing tea; she was frightened his open wounds would infect our cats.

But her chair had its back to the door. She often didn't see him poke his head round. He would look at her, to make sure she hadn't seen him, then look at me, in mute appeal for masculine solidarity. I would give him an imperceptible nod, and he would eat from the saucers, with a quick glance up at her back, every so often. Then he would slink, utterly weary and beaten, into the cat basket, pulling the white wire door to after him, and sink into exhausted slumber.

Poor old sod, magnificent though he was, the world was getting too much for him; like that old gunfighter in the westerns that knows his time is nearly up, and would like a bit of peace before the end.

I often considered adopting him, on such dreadful nights. It would have meant sending him to be neutered, and he might have enjoyed a few years of comfort before the end, sleek and warm and not bleeding any more, the fur grown back over the wounds. But who was I to interfere with a free spirit of such dignity? Would he have thanked me? And perhaps he was somebody else's cat? He certainly wasn't wild; he had beautiful manners; never sprayed in our house; let me stroke his unwounded parts with grave condescension when we met. A realist. I used to lie in bed on wild nights, glad to know he was full and sleeping in the warmth of my kitchen. I was sorry, last year, when he never came, and we knew he'd fought his last fight.

Sir Thomas Tallis, the spotless tabby, on the other hand, while a full tom, is a profitable coward. He hasn't got a scar on him. He is an intelligent cat, intelligent enough to be a female.

He has worked out that it doesn't pay to be in a hurry. He sits and watches the other toms slug it out, the black and ginger fur rolling across the shed roof like autumn leaves. Then, when they have shot their bolts and gone home to tea, he moves in with profit. Our she-cats like him. He has a handsome sharp delicate face, and you could almost mistake him for a female, but for the macho hips. He is much more gentle with them than the others, and has at least one litter to his credit, so his style works. He is a great waiter, sitting in the drain in the cranny by the back door, even on the coldest nights. He will let you pick him up, though he doesn't like it much. You can, with persistence, get him to purr in your arms. The only trouble is, he's painfully thin, under very greasy fur, so he isn't a great pleasure to hold. Again, I am tempted to adopt him and neuter him; he'd make a lovely clean, plump neuter. But I have no more right to neuter him than he has to neuter me. I just wish they'd feed him more at home, and give him a bath occasionally.

The last cat, Thomas Gresty, ginger and white, is totally unpopular. He is a bully, and in between mating, beats our she-cats up unmercifully, till they scream (all except Sheba). But that was before the girls set up the Home Guard. Now, in the evenings, they sit patiently by the cat-flap, two each side of it. They sit for hours, as if they were mousing at a mouse-hole. Waiting for Gresty. They have sussed out that the most powerful tom is helpless at the moment he puts his head through the cat-flap. Even worse for Gresty, he tries to pull his head back too quickly, and the flap jams round his neck and he's stuck there, while four or even eight female paws flail at him. I wonder he hasn't lost an eye; it's a real bloodbath. But I have no sympathy. He is a coward, without dignity. As he comes across our shed roof, he looks in at the kitchen window, with big terror-filled eyes. He is watching out for *me*. And this brings out the tom-cat in me. I glare back at him; he stares transfixed, terrified, unable to break away from my glare. I look deep into his mean, bullying, cowardly soul, which is as empty as a cardboard box. Then he starts to lick his lips uneasily. So I open my mouth in a cat-snarl and hiss at him through the window-glass. He cowers, and turns sideways, flicking glances towards the safety of home. I start my horrible tom-cat caterwauling, a perfect imitation and the loudest ever heard in the village. His back is twitching . . . he's at breaking-point. I give a last heart-rending attack-scream and leap into the air, both arms upraised.

He flees ignominiously. All my she-cats, who have been watching with the deepest interest, look at me with warm approving eyes. I am their hero.

All this happens while I am there. What happens when I am not? I hear the cat-flap banging in the night, every ten minutes or so at irregular intervals. Every so often, the foolish Bella tries to sharpen her claws on the silver cover of the ironing board, which always falls on her head with a terrible bang that rocks the house. I hear the chair-legs going bang-bang, bang-bang on the hard tile floor; that's a chase setting up; I hear another Biro ting into goal, under the convector-heater. Oh, for a spyhole in the kitchen wall! What dramas, what love-scenes, what comedies and tragedies!

But they need their privacy and I need my sleep.

THE SINGING CAT

STEVIE SMITH

It was a little captive cat
    Upon a crowded train
His mistress takes him from his box
    To ease his fretful pain.

She holds him tight upon her knee
    The graceful animal
And all the people look at him
    He is so beautiful.

But oh he pricks and oh he prods
    And turns upon her knee
Then lifteth up his innocent voice
    In plaintive melody.

He lifteth up his innocent voice
    He lifteth up, he singeth
And to each human countenance
    A smile of grace he bringeth.

He lifteth up his innocent paw
    Upon her breast he clingeth
And everybody cries, Behold
    The cat, the cat that singeth.

He lifteth up his innocent voice
    He lifteth up, he singeth
And all the people warm themselves
    In the love his beauty bringeth.

KEEPING UP STANDARDS

J. K. HUYSMANS

THIS ANIMAL was affectionate and winning, but wily. She would not permit any deviation, she intended that one should get up and that one should go to bed at the same time. When she was discontent, she expressed in the darkness of her look nuances of irritation which her master never mistook. If he returned before eleven o'clock at night, she was waiting for him at the door, in the entrance hall, scratching the wood, miaowing before he had entered the room! Then she would roll her languorous pupils of greeny-gold, rub herself against his breeches, jump on the furniture, stand herself upright to look like a small horse rearing, and when he came near her, give him — in friendship — great blows with her head. If it were after eleven o'clock she did not go up to him, but restricted herself to getting up only when he came near her, still arching her back but not caressing him. If it were later still, she would not move and she would complain grumblingly if he allowed himself to smooth the top of her head or scratch the underneath of her neck . . .

RITUAL

ROBERT WESTALL

WITH JEOFFREY, ritual is far more than when you get up and when you go to bed. On first entering the kitchen in the morning, he paces the table, demanding five minutes of tail pulling. Then he will accompany me to the bathroom, drinking at the plug-hole of the basin, circumnavigating the edge of the bath while I am in it and mousing the hem of the bath towel while I stand freezing and shivering. While I prepare breakfast, he demands his "special" drink of water, in a red dish-lid, though fresh water has been down on the floor for the other cats all night.

At breakfast, he refuses to let me read, dashing the newspaper from my hands by main force, and lying on it to settle the argument. Breakfast's free hand is for tummy-tickling.

At nine, I get a little peace when he departs to Number 8, to finish off their cats' breakfast, have his tail pulled again, and nap for exactly half an hour on the best chintz bedspread.

Mid-morning brings the possibility of gardening at Number 6 or Number 3; he prefers weeding, when he can pounce on the flying soil, but pruning of shrubs and bushes is very popular. If no gardening is in progress, then he waits for cars to park, greeting their emerging owners by throwing himself over on his back and waving his legs in the air.

Should the family in the adjoining back garden have tea outside, he is there, formal, polite. Then for tea back home, when he insists on licking the top of the new cat food tin before the food is shared out. After his meal he will have a nap on the high shelves of the kitchen, reaching them by way of a human shoulder, which he summons with a flick of his eyes. About eight o'clock, he descends to choose between several laps, only deigning to settle after presenting his rear end to have his tail pulled exactly four times.

Should he meet you in the hall, there must be at least five minutes of pretending to be a mouse with your fingers, on the treads of the open-plan stair.

And so on to getting supper, and his last ceremonial drink of "special" water (never more than three sips). The whole day is ritualized, and I dare say had I the time and patience and intelligence to read his signals, every second of the day would be taken up with some little ceremony . . .

Given such catty charisma, and such catty enthusiasm for ritual, is it any wonder that cats are fascinated by large human institutions? But it's the effects they have . . . it's as if Ancient Egypt is always threatening to happen again.

CATS AND INSTITUTIONS

MIKE

SIR ERNEST A. WALLIS BUDGE

The cat who assisted in keeping the main gate of the British Museum
from February 1909 to January 1929

I N THE days when that famous and learned man, Sir Richard Garnett, ruled over the Department of Printed Books in the British Museum, he was frequently visited by a cat who was generally known among the staff as "Black Jack".

He was a very handsome black creature, with a white shirt front and white paws, and whiskers of great length. He was fond of sitting on the desks in the Reading Room, and he never hesitated to ask a reader to hold open both folding doors when he wanted to go out into the corridor. Being shut in one of the newspaper rooms one Sunday, and being bored, he amused himself by sharpening his claws on the bindings of the volumes of newspapers, and it must be confessed did much damage. This brought down upon him the wrath of the officials, and he was banished from the library; the Clerk of the Works was ordered to get rid of him, and tried to do so, but failed, for Black Jack had disappeared mysteriously. The truth was that two of the members of the staff arranged for him to be kept in safety in a certain place, and provided him with food and milk. An official report was written to the effect that Black Jack had disappeared, and he was "presumed dead"; the bindings of the volumes of newspapers were repaired, and the official mind was once more at peace. A few weeks later Black Jack reappeared, and everyone was delighted to see him again; and the chief officials asked no questions.

Early in the spring of 1908 the Keeper of the Egyptian Cat Mummies in the British Museum was going down the steps of his official residence, when he saw Black Jack coming towards the steps and carrying something rather large in his mouth. He came to the steps and deposited his burden on the steps at the Keeper's feet and then turned and walked solemnly away. The something which he deposited on the steps was a kitten, and that kitten was later known to fame as "Mike". The kitten was taken in and cared for and grew and flourished, and by great good luck was adopted as a pal by the two cats already in the house. So all was well.

When Mike was a little older he went and made friends with the kind-hearted gatekeeper at the main gate, and he began to frequent the lodge. By day and night he was always sure of a welcome, and thus he was the happy possessor of two homes. On Sunday mornings the house cat taught him to stalk pigeons in the colonnade. Mike was set to "point" like a dog, and the house cat little by little drove the pigeons up into a corner. The pigeons became dazed, and fell down, and then each cat seized a bird and carried it into the house uninjured. The Housekeeper took the pigeons from the cats, and in return for them gave a slice of beef or mutton and milk to each cat. The pigeons were taken into a little side room, and after they had eaten some maize and drunk water, they flew out of the window none the worse for their handling by the cats. The fact was that neither cat liked to eat game with dirty, sooty, feathers on it; they preferred clean, cooked meat.

As time went on, Mike, wishing to keep his proceedings during the hours of night uncriticized by the household, preferred the lodge to the house, and finally he took up his abode there, the corner shelf out of the draughts was prepared for him to sleep on and he could go out and come in at any time he pleased both by day and by night. The Keeper of the Mummied Cats took care to feed him during the lean years of the war, and whoever went short, Mike did not. During the last two years he was difficult to feed because of his decaying teeth, but a diet of tender meat and fish on alternate days kept him going. He preferred sole to whiting, and whiting to haddock, and sardines to herrings; for cod he had no use whatever. He owed much to the three kind-hearted gatekeepers who cooked his food for him, and treated him as a man and a brother.

70

ROOM 8 – THE CLASSROOM CAT

GYLES BRANDRETH

ROOM 8 was an American tabby and white tom cat who one day in 1953 turned up at Elysian Heights Elementary School in Baxter St., Los Angeles. He wandered round the classrooms, enjoying titbits from the children's lunches, and for some reason seemed to have a preference for Room 8 – hence his name.

He turned up faithfully for lessons every day, even when it was pouring down with rain. In the evenings, and in school holidays, he vanished, and no one knew where he went.

The cat became the school mascot, loved by pupils and staff alike for his kindly nature. He never minded being fussed over by the children, but seemed to enjoy the attention, and as time went on he became widely known as a character. He appeared several times on television, and a book was written about him. Royalties from the book about Room 8 and gifts of money enclosed in fan mail were used to boost the school's library fund. He attended Elysian Heights for fifteen years, and during this time received more than 10,000 letters, mostly from children but some purporting to be from other cats. They were dutifully answered by sixth-grade students who signed them all with a special paw-print stamp.

In later years Room 8 was looked after in the school holidays by a family who lived near the school and whose four children attended it, but he was fed at school in term time by specially appointed "feeders" among the pupils.

Sadly, all good things come to an end, and the cat who had seen countless children all through their schooldays died in 1968, aged approximately twenty-two, of kidney failure. Because of his great popularity a Room 8 fund was established after his death and used to maintain a children's bed at a Los Angeles orthopaedic hospital. Gifts of books, magazine subscriptions and so on are still sent to the school in Room 8's name, to the benefit of the pupils now there. It is a fitting memorial to this dearly loved cat that his memory should be kept alive by gifts which benefit children after his death.

CHURCH CATS

MARGARET ELLIS

THERE WERE for a long time three black and white cats – a father and two sons – attached to the church of St Mary Abbots, Kensington.

When an organ builder to whom they had belonged left the neighbourhood, they installed themselves outside the church, attracted by the warmth of the paving stones which were heated by boilers below. A kindly verger, Mr Reginald Racher, gave them food and drink.

The saga with which I am concerned began one icy morning when the vicar, the late Prebendary Eley (subsequently Bishop of Gibraltar), arriving to take early service, found one of the cats lying stretched out, stiff with cold, on the pavement. The boilers below had failed, and the cat appeared to be dead. Indeed, he would have died if the vicar had not taken him indoors and fed him with teaspoonfuls of egg whipped up with brandy.

Restored to health, the cat was given the name Thomas Aquinas. His brother, because he was of a somewhat timid disposition, was called Thomas Didymus: it was only after some time that this cat ventured inside the church, but having done so he made himself at home. The father, who was named Thomas à Kempis, never went into the church. The verger built him a house outside and saw that he was fed and cared for.

St Mary Abbots church was infested with mice: they even nibbled the candle-wax in the sanctuary. Thomas Aquinas and Thomas Didymus put this to rights. They smelt the mice and heard them scampering below a grille in the floor, above the furnace. Sometimes they could see a mouse through the bars of the grille, but were unable to get at it. Eventually they contrived to find a way down. The slaughter was on a vast scale. Yet out of all those mice the cats not only spared one, but made a friend of him. This mouse used to be fed on cake and biscuits in the vestry, in the company of the cats, and when the verger was serving in the sanctuary he would see the mouse sitting up, a yard or so away.

Nor was it unusual during service for one cat or both to sit respectfully in the sanctuary. Or they might choose a position from which they could look up at the royal pew – at Princess Alice, Princess Marina, or Princess Margaret.

On Thursdays at 11.30am a Communion service was held in the chapel of St Paul: because there were no steps it was convenient for elderly persons. Among those who attended was a Miss Bell who was particularly fond of the cats. Each Thursday, on their own initiative, the two cats used to take up their positions one at each end of the pew in which Miss Bell sat. While she went to the altar they remained behind with perfect decorum.

When Miss Bell died the cats met the coffin, walked ahead of it up the cloister that leads into the church, and, when it was placed on trestles and covered with a pall, sat underneath, remaining there through the night. Next morning, as the cortège moved down the aisle, the cats were sitting on the radiators to either side of the door.

The cats participated fully in the life of the church. At a baptism they would move among the people, giving particular pleasure to the children. At weddings, Thomas Aquinas had a way of sidling between the bride-to-be and her father as they went up the aisle. Then the two cats would slip away and appear again outside on the pavement among the guests, when the bride and bridegroom were getting into their car.

Over the Christmas period they sat in the crib, in the hay, eyes glinting. A child was heard to exclaim: "Why! they're *real* animals!" For days the cats' fur smelt of hay. Parishioners brought them Christmas gifts: packets of cat's food – even a small roast chicken!

Inevitably there were those who objected to cats in a church. For a while an effort was made to discourage the Thomas brothers, but it was a half-hearted gesture. Most of the congregation liked them.

Besides, they were not in church all the time. Thomas Aquinas used to take himself off to Peter's Eating House, which was close to the entrance of St Mary Abbots, where he was made much of and fed on steak. Or he would cross Church Street – looking to right and to left – to the "Prince of Wales", where he enjoyed a sip of beer. The proprietor threatened one day that he would have to send in a bill to cover Thomas's drinks!

One of the verger's tasks was to count the collection. He did this in the vestry, arranging the coins in neat piles, coppers, sixpences, shillings, florins and so on. Thomas Aquinas and Thomas Didymus would sit on the table watching. Then suddenly out would come a paw, scattering the coins like a child overturning a tower of bricks!

The pulpit was a forbidden area. One day the congregation was waiting for the service to begin, the loudspeaker set for a visiting preacher, when a rhythmic sound began to fill the church – growing to a crescendo, then abating, only to increase again. People did not know what to think. Then the verger had his suspicions. Sure enough, Thomas Aquinas had found his way into the pulpit and was purring full strength into the microphone.

ABNER OF THE PORCH

GEOFFREY HOUSEHOLD

WHEN MY voice broke, even Abner and MacGillivray understood my grief. I did not expect sympathy from MacGillivray, for he had no reason to like me. But he knew what it was to be excluded from cathedral ceremonies. He was the Bishop's dog.

Abner was masterless. I would not claim that he appreciated the alto's solo in the Magnificat when the organ was hushed and there was no other sound in the million and a half cubic feet of the Cathedral but the slender purity of a boy's voice; yet he would patronize me after such occasions with air of the master alto which he might have been. Though not a full Tom, he knew the ancestral songs which resemble our own. To our ears the scale of cats is distasteful, but one cannot deny them sustained notes of singular loveliness and clarity.

Abner's career had followed a common human pattern. My father was the gardener, responsible for the shaven lawns and discreet flower beds of the cathedral close. Some three years earlier he had suffered from an invasion of moles – creatures of ecclesiastical subtlety who avoided all the crude traps set for them by a mere layman. The cat, appearing from nowhere, took an interest. After a week he had caught the lot, laying out his game-bag each morning upon the tarpaulin which covered the mower.

Fed and praised by my father, he began to pay some attention to public relations and attracted the attention of visitors. Officially recognized as an ornament of the Cathedral when his photograph appeared in the local paper, he ventured to advance from the lawns and tombstones to the porch. There he captivated the Dean, always politely rising from the stone bench and thrusting his noble flanks against the gaitered leg. He was most gracious to the Bishop and the higher clergy, but he would only stroke the Dean. He knew very well from bearing and tone of voice, gentle though they were, that the Cathedral belonged to him. It was the Dean who christened him Abner.

To such a personage the dog of our new Bishop was a disaster. MacGillivray was of respectable middle age, and had on occasion a sense of dignity; but when dignity was not called for he behaved like any other Aberdeen terrier and would race joyously round the Cathedral or across the close, defying whatever human being was in charge of him to catch the lead which bounced and flew behind.

His first meeting with his rival set the future tone of their relations. He ventured with appalling temerity to make sport of the cathedral cat. Abner stretched himself, yawned, allowed MacGillivray's charge to approach within a yard, leaped to the narrow and rounded top of a tombstone and, draping himself over it, went ostentatiously to sleep. MacGillivray jumped and yapped at the tail tip which graciously waved for him, and then realized that he was being treated as a puppy. After that the two passed each other politely but without remark. In our closed world of the Cathedral such coolness between servants of Dean and servants of Bishop was familiar.

MacGillivray considered that he should be on permanent duty with his master. Since he was black, small and ingenious, it was difficult to prevent him. So devoted a friend could not be cruelly chained – and in summer the French windows of the Bishop's Palace were always open.

He first endeared himself to choir and clergy at the ceremony of the Bishop's installation. Magnificent in mitre and full robes, the Bishop at the head of his procession knocked with his crozier upon the Cathedral door to demand admission. MacGillivray, observing that his master was shut out and in need of help, hurtled across the close, bounced at the door and added his excited barks to the formal solemnity of the Bishop's order.

Led away in disapproving silence, he took the enormity of his crime more seriously than we did. On his next appearance he behaved with decent humility, following the unconscious Bishop down the chancel and into the pulpit with bowed head and tail well below the horizontal.

Such anxious piety was even more embarrassing than bounce. It became my duty, laid upon me by the Bishop in person, to ensure on all formal occasions that MacGillivray had not evaded the butler and was safely confined. I was even empowered to tie him up to the railings on the north side of the close in cases of emergency.

I do not think the Bishop ever realized what was troubling his friend and erring brother, MacGillivray – normally a dog of sense who could mind his own business however great his affection for his master. When he accompanied the Bishop around the diocese he never committed the solecism of entering a parish church and never used the vicar's cat as an objective for assault practice.

His indiscipline at home was, we were all sure, due to jealousy of Abner. He resented with Scottish obstinacy the fact that he was ejected in disgrace from the Cathedral whereas Abner was not. He could not be expected to understand that Abner's discreet movements were beyond human control.

The Dean could and did quite honestly declare that he had never seen that cat in the Cathedral. Younger eyes, however, which knew where to look, had often distinguished Abner curled up on the ornate stone canopy over the tomb of a seventeenth-century admiral. In winter he would sometimes sleep upon the left arm of a stone crusader in the cavity between shield and mailed shirt – a dank spot, I thought, until I discovered that it captured a current of warm air from the grating beside the effigy. In both his resting-places he was, if he chose to be, invisible. He was half Persian, tiger-striped with brownish grey on lighter grey, and he matched the stone of the Cathedral.

As the summer went by, the feud between Abner and MacGillivray became more subtle. Both scored points. MacGillivray, if he woke up feeling youthful, used to chase the tame pigeons in the close. One morning, to the surprise of both dog and bird, a pigeon failed to get out of the way in time and broke a wing. MacGillivray was embarrassed. He sniffed the pigeon, wagged his tail to show that there was no ill feeling and sat down to think.

Abner strolled from the porch and held down the pigeon with a firm, gentle paw. He picked it up in his mouth and presented it with liquid and appealing eyes to an elegant American tourist who was musing sentimentally in the close. She swore that the cat had asked her to heal the bird – which, by remaining a whole week in our town in and out of the vet's consulting room, she did. Personally I think that Abner was attracted by the feline grace of her walk and was suggesting that, as the pigeon could be of no more use to the Cathedral, she might as well eat it. But whatever his motives he had again made MacGillivray look a clumsy and impulsive fool.

MacGillivray's revenge was a little primitive. He deposited bones and offal in dark corners of the porch and pretended that Abner had put them there. That was the second worst crime he knew – to leave on a human floor the inedible portions of his meals.

The verger was deceived and submitted a grave complaint in writing to the Dean. The Dean, however, knew very well that Abner had no interest in mutton bones, old or new. He was familiar with the cat's tastes. Indeed it was rumoured from the Deanery that he secreted a little box in his pocket at meals, into which he would drop such delicacies as the head of a small trout or the liver of a roast duck.

I cannot remember all the incidents of the cold war. And, any way, I could not swear to their truth. My father and the Dean read into the animals' behaviour motives which were highly unlikely and then shamelessly embroidered them, creating a whole miscellany of private legend for the canons and the choir. So I will only repeat the triumph of MacGillivray and its sequel, both of which I saw myself.

That fulfilment of every dog's dream appeared at first final and over-whelming victory. It was September 1st, the feast of St. Giles, our patron saint. Evensong was a full choral and instrumental service, traditional, exquisite, and attracting a congregation whose interest was in music rather than religion. The Bishop was to preach. Perhaps the effort of composition, of appealing to well-read intellectuals without offending the simpler clergy, had created an atmosphere of hard work and anxiety in the Bishop's study. At any rate MacGillivray was nervous and mischievous.

While I was ensuring his comfort before shutting him up, he twitched the lead out of my hand and was off on his quarter-mile course round the Cathedral looking for a private entrance. When at last I caught him, the changes of the bells had stopped. I had only five minutes before the processional entry of the choir. There wasn't even time to race across the close and tie him up to the railings.

I rushed into the north transept with MacGillivray under my arm, pushed him down the stairs into the crypt and shut the door behind him. I knew that he could not get out. Our Norman crypt was closed to visitors during the service, and no one on a summer evening would have reason to go down to the masons' and carpenters' stores, the strong-room or the boilers. All I feared was that MacGillivray's yaps might be heard through the gratings in the Cathedral floor.

I dived into my ruffled surplice and took my place in the procession, earning the blackest possible looks from the choirmaster. I just had time to explain to him that it was the fault of MacGillivray. I was not forgiven, but the grin exchanged between choirmaster and Precentor suggested that I probably would be – if I wasn't still panting by the time that the alto had to praise all famous men and our fathers that begat us.

St. Giles, if he still had any taste for earthly music, must have approved of his servants that evening. The Bishop, always an effective preacher, surpassed himself. His sinewy arguments were of course beyond me. But I had my eye – vain little beast that I was – on the music critics from the London papers, and I could see that several of them were so interested that they were bursting to take over the pulpit and reply.

Only once did he falter, when the barking of MacGillivray, hardly perceptible to anyone but his master and me, caught the episcopal ear. Even then his momentary hesitation was put down to a search for the right word.

I felt that my desperate disposal of MacGillivray might not be appreciated. He must have been audible to any of the congregation sitting near the gratings of the northern aisle. So I shot down to release him immediately after the recessional. The noise was startling as soon as I opened the door. MacGillivray was holding the stairs against a stranger in the crypt.

The man was good-dogging him and trying to make him shut up. He had a small suit-case by his side. When two sturdy vergers, attracted by the noise, appeared hot on my heels, the intruder tried to bolt – dragging behind him MacGillivray with teeth closed on the turn-up of his trousers. We detained him and opened the suit-case. It contained twenty pounds weight of the Cathedral silver. During the long service our massive but primitive strong room door had been expertly opened.

The congregation was dispersing, but Bishop, Dean, Archdeacon and innumerable canons were still in the Cathedral. They attended the excitement just as any other crowd. Under the circumstances MacGillivray was the centre of the most complimentary fuss. The canons would have genially petted any dog. But this was the Bishop's dog. The wings of gowns and surplices flowed over him like those of exclamatory seagulls descending upon a stranded fish.

Dignity was represented only by our local superintendent of police and the terrier himself. When the thief had been led away MacGillivray reverently followed his master out of the Cathedral; his whole attitude reproached us for ever dreaming that he might take advantage of his popularity.

At the porch, however, he turned round and loosed one short, triumphant bark into the empty nave. The Bishop's chaplain unctuously suggested that it was a little voice of thanksgiving. So it was – but far from pious. I noticed where MacGillivray's muzzle was pointing. That bark was for a softness of outline, a shadow, a striping of small stone pinnacles upon the canopy of the Admiral's Tomb.

For several days – all of ten I should say – Abner deserted both the Cathedral and its porch. He then returned to his first friend, helping my father to make the last autumn cut of the grass and offering his catch of small game for approval. The Dean suggested that he was in need of sunshine. My father shook his head and said nothing. It was obvious to both of us that for Abner the Cathedral had been momentarily defiled. He reminded me of an old verger who gave in his resignation – it was long overdue any way – after discovering a family party eating lunch from paper bags in the Lady Chapel.

He went back to the porch a little before the Harvest Festival, for he always enjoyed that. During a whole week while the decorations were in place he could find a number of discreet lairs where it was impossible to detect his presence. There may also have been a little hunting in the night. We did not attempt to fill the vastness of the Cathedral with all the garden produce dear to a parish church, but the Dean was fond of fat sheaves of wheat, oats and barley, bound round the middle like sheaves on a heraldic shield.

It was his own festival in his own Cathedral, so that he, not the Bishop, conducted it. He had made the ritual as enjoyable as that of Christmas, reviving ancient customs for which he was always ready to quote authority. I suspect that medieval deans would have denied his interpretation of their scanty records, but they would have recognized a master of stage management.

His most effective revival was a procession of cathedral tenants and benefactors, each bearing some offering in kind which the Dean received on the altar steps. Fruit, honey and cakes were common, always with some touch of magnificence in the quality, quantity or container. On one occasion the landlord of the Pilgrim's Inn presented a roasted peacock set in jelly with tail feathers erect. There was some argument about this on the grounds that it ran close to advertisement. But the Dean would not be dissuaded. He insisted that any craftsman had the right to present a unique specimen of his skill.

That year the gifts were more humble. My father, as always, led the procession with a basket tray upon which was a two-foot bunch of black grapes from the vinery in the Canons' garden. A most original participant was a dear old nursery gardener who presented a plant of his new dwarf camellia which had been the botanical sensation of the year and could not yet be bought for money. There was also a noble milk-pan of Alpine strawberries and cream – which, we hoped, the Cathedral School would share next day with the Alms Houses.

While the file of some twenty persons advanced into the chancel, the choir full-bloodedly sang the 65th Psalm to the joyous score of our own organist. The Dean's sense of theatre was as faultless as ever. Lavish in ritual and his own vestments, he then played his part with the utmost simplicity. He thanked and blessed each giver almost conversationally.

Last in the procession were four boys of the Cathedral School bearing a great silver bowl of nuts gathered in the hedgerows. The gift and their movements were traditional. As they separated, two to the right and two to the left, leaving the Dean alone upon the altar steps, a shadow appeared at his feet and vanished so swiftly that by the time our eyes had registered its true, soft shape it was no longer there.

The Dean bent down and picked up a dead field-mouse. He was not put

out of countenance for a moment. He laid it reverently with the other gifts.
No one was present to be thanked; but when the Dean left the Cathedral
after service and stopped in the porch to talk to Abner he was – to the
surprise of the general public – still wearing his full vestments, stiff,
gorgeous and suggesting the power of the Church to protect and armour
with its blessings the most humble of its servants.

THE MONASTERY CAT

JOYCE STRANGER

THE MONASTERY was perched on a cliff, high in the mountains. In summer the holy Fathers looked down from an eagle perch on sweeping columns of dark pine trees which stretched all the way to the distant village huddled in a valley, where steep roofs were aligned to shed the winter snow.

In winter the world was masked with white. The sun glittered on sheets of snow. There was no relief from the stark lack of colour.

It was quiet in the monastery.

The days passed without incident. The holy Fathers rose early to pray, before starting the day's work. Father Anselm was in charge of the goats who provided milk and butter and cheese. Often he wished that there were other animals. He was a farmer's son and he hungered for the care of a herd of cows; for sheep; for dogs to lighten the day, and most of all a cat.

But he dared not ask for a cat.

Father Jerome was in charge of the gardens where he grew all the vegetables that were needed. He too liked animals, and missed them, so that often he helped milk the goats, and enjoyed working in the big sheds where the three nannies lived. Each year the farmer in the village brought his Billy up the mountain, and each year there were three kids to liven the days. Some years there were twins.

The Fathers never left the monastery. They watched the eagle soar high above them; they watched the ant people in the village below. They had little chance to sin. Their sins were sins of anger, and of envy; of greed, when food became all-important as there was so little to mark the passing days; of spite against one another, living too close together, being human, and not saints, as they would have wished.

Their pleasure came from song. Sometimes, on a very clear day, the villagers could hear the Fathers singing, and the sonorous notes of the organ, drifting down the mountains, sounded like a choir of angels, high above them. They paused to listen and to smile at one another.

The villagers also heard the monastery bell. It marked the hours and it was rung for meals, and the villagers timed their clocks by it. Its silver chime sounded over the village like a benison, and the notes floated on the air.

Life in the monastery had gone on unchanging for so long that sometimes Father Anselm wondered if he were becoming mummified. Longings for the world outside assailed him and he had to confess that he was not entirely tuned to the holy life that he should be leading. He had been very young when he joined the Order.

And now he was growing old and wondered if he had truly found his vocation.

The longing for animals was so strong that he spent more time than was necessary among the goats. Each one was a character, and he had named them all. He grieved when they died and he rejoiced when the kids were born, thanking God for the repeated miracle of life.

One winter morning he left the goats and walked slowly across the snow-covered yard. He felt rebellious, and longed to open the gate and stride down the mountain and snatch some of the life that he had missed. Shock at his thoughts stopped him in mid-stride and he looked up at the blue sky and prayed that the Lord would forgive him for his frailty.

He would go into the chapel and pray for his restlessness to leave him.

The tiny chapel was beside the big gate. That was rarely opened. It blocked out the world, a massive oak gate, thick-planked and iron-studded. Sometimes it reminded him of a prison door.

Outside the gate, a baby cried.

Shocked, Father Anselm stood and stared. Surely no one had brought a child to the holy Fathers. What on earth would they do? The cry came again, a long wailing sobbing call that brought some of the other Fathers running. Father Anselm opened the gate.

There in the snow was not a baby, but a tiny Siamese kitten. Its small back was bloodstained; its blue eyes stared up at them and it wailed pitifully.

"What man has done this?" Father Jerome asked angrily.

Father Anselm looked at the unmarked snow. He looked upwards, at the eagle soaring above.

"No man," he said.

"Are you suggesting this is a miracle?" Father Jacques asked in a shocked voice. He was writing a book about miracles, and saw the hand of God in many ways; but not in the advent of a battered kitten from outer space.

"The eagle snatched it and dropped it," Father Anselm said. "Perhaps God had a hand in it too. He moves in mysterious ways."

He lifted the kitten and Father Jerome closed the great gate.

The talons had cut deep, but the kitten was strong. He purred and rubbed his small head against Father Anselm's cheek, and the monk knew at once that he could not part with this morsel of life. He was afraid the Abbot would forbid them to keep the kitten, but the Abbot came to look, and touched the small creature and smiled.

"He came to us for succour and that he will have," he said.

Father Anselm dressed the injuries with the ointment that he had bought from the apothecary for one of the goats; he fed him with bread and milk, and he found a wooden box in a corner of the goat shed and scrubbed it clean.

Father Jerome remembered that there were old blankets in the big armoire on the stairs of the passage that led to the monks' spartan cells. He cut one of the worst worn into pieces, and he found a stone bottle and filled it with warm water. The little cat would be suffering from shock.

The kitten did not intend to sleep in his box.

He had been snatched from his mother, as he played in the sun; he had been carried miles into the air, the great talons digging cruelly into his fur. He had summoned all his strength and twisted upwards and slashed with needle-like claws at the bird's feathered legs and had drawn blood. The eagle, startled by the unexpected attack, had dropped his prey.

Father Anselm looked at the kitten. He was about three months old; his fur was cream; his paws and tail and mask were a delicate grey-blue; his eyes were as vivid as the gentians that grew in the summer pastures.

They named him Ciel because he had dropped from the sky.

Ciel soon became part of the monastery's routine. His small agile body was to be seen trotting busily along the passages; exploring the cells, visiting each monk in turn, giving some his favours by day, and others by night. The box and the blanket remained by the big fire in the kitchen, but the Fathers kept Ciel's night-time visits a dark secret. He slept now on one bed, now on another, and those who were honoured by his visits spent idle moments teasing him with a straw, on which he pounced, or pulling their rope girdles along the ground, watching him dart like quicksilver.

There was often laughter among the monks as Ciel danced with his shadow, or pounced on imaginary  mice. He loved to leap on to the big dresser, or to the top of the armoire, and jump on to the unwary as they passed beneath so that when there was a sudden startled shout the brothers laughed and looked at one another and said,

"Oh that Ciel. He's done it again."

Ciel killed the rats that lived even here on the mountain, attracted by the stored sacks of food. He killed the mice, and the monastery had never been so free from vermin.

"He earns his place," Father Anselm often said. The monks repeated themselves on many occasions as there was so little to discuss.

Ciel even invaded the chapel but here he seemed to know he must not make a noise or play. He curled himself neatly on a pew and listened to the singing. He loved song, and sometimes, very wickedly, Father Anselm sang one of his boyhood ballads, songs of knights and ladies, and of rivers flowing swiftly through green fields; of lakes and of pastures, and he sang the song his grandfather had sung when milking the cows. He often sang it to the goats to bring their milk more swiftly.

Kitty coo, kitty coo, kitty coo milking,

Let down your milk, let down your milk,
Kitty coo, milking.

Ciel would lie on his knee and look up at him wide-eyed, intent, with a stare that seemed to lay bare his soul. Then the monk would laugh and tickle the cat and the cat would turn on his back and attack the big brown fist in mock battle, pretending to scratch and stab, but always keeping the long lethal claws sheathed.

Sometimes he rode on Father Anselm's shoulder. He did this for no one else and some of the monks were just a little jealous, enticing the cat with titbits from their plates, and even lifting him to sit beside their ears, but Ciel would have none of that.

He went his own way, and no one could change him.

He had been with the monks three years. He had learned that every meal time was heralded by the sound of the bell, and he knew that then the holy Fathers left their chores and took their wooden dishes and went to the cook for their portions. They fed sparsely, on porridge and rye bread for breakfast; on a stew of vegetables with very little meat at lunch, with rye bread and cheese for dessert; and at supper they dined on eggs and bread and drank the goats' milk.

Ciel shared their food, and when the long procession filed through the corridors towards the refectory, the little cat led it, marching sedately, tail

erect, occasionally looking back to see that everyone was following him.
Even the Abbot had to laugh at their leader, and his small self-assurance, and
no one knew that sometimes when the wind blew eerily round the corners,
alarming the little cat, Ciel found his way to the Abbot's warm room, where
the old man slept for so little a while. He would spend half the night in
prayer, with a small furry body tucked against his knees, under his robes,
hiding from the wind, delighted to find a human awake and able to protect
him from the invisible demons that strode outside the monastery walls,
yelling their anger.

One morning the bell rang, and no cat appeared. The holy Fathers stared
at one another. Who had seen him last? Where had he spent the night?
Only then did they find that Ciel distributed his favours impartially and at
one time or another had slept on every bed in the monastery. But that night
no one had seen him. No one had seen him since supper the day before.

They searched the monastery. It was so easy for a little cat bent on
mischief to run before them and hide. They searched the cupboards and the
goat shed; they searched their drawers and their small possessions; they
stared at the great gate, wondering if Ciel could have climbed it and gone
outside.

But it was winter and there were no tracks in the snow.

Father Anselm looked up.

The eagle was soaring overhead.

He shook his fist at the devil bird. There was their answer. The kitten
they had saved three years ago had fallen victim in the end.

There were no smiles on the bearded faces, and the voices that sang that
day were sad. Father Anselm moved the little box; Father Jerome hid the
small dish that always held Ciel's food. Fathers in every cell in the monastery

hid the telltale pieces of string with which they played with the cat.

The solemn procession that led down the corridor to the refectory moved slowly, as if at a funeral, and the Abbot chided himself for missing so small a part of his routine. It was only a cat . . .

But they thought they saw Ciel dancing with his shadow and they heard his wails.

Three days passed.

Father Anselm still longed for the cat. He missed the muscular little body that raced through the shadows, or played in the goat shed, or leaped from the cupboards. He still thought he could hear wails and chided himself for an over-active imagination.

Breakfast was over on the third day and all the monks were about their daily business. The bell would not sound again until lunch-time.

The villagers too were about their daily business, the men at their work, the women chatting as they shopped for the family's food.

It would be two hours before the chime sounded on the mountain.

Suddenly they heard the bell.

The schoolchildren ran outside and stared up at the monastery. The shopkeepers and the women raced into the village street, for this was no silver chime, but an angry clang clang that went on and on endlessly.

Was the monastery on fire?

Had a monk died, and another monk, overcome by grief, gone mad as he clanged the angry bell?

There was no smoke.

There was no sign of turmoil.

But there was turmoil.

Father Anselm left the goat in mid-milking and she kicked the bucket over and flooded her pen. Father Jerome dropped the bucket of water he was carrying and injured his toe. The Abbot, at prayer, stood suddenly and knocked over his precious cup, the only possession that he had brought from the world outside. It was a very ordinary cup, but he was sad when it broke as it was a link with a childhood he had almost forgotten.

The cook forgot the stew and left the flame too high.

The monks ran.

They picked up their skirts and raced to the bell room, and counted heads as they ran. All were there. So who was ringing the bell? Had the devil come in person to punish them for wickedness? Or was there a demon or hobgoblin there in the empty room?

They stopped at the door, afraid to go in. The Abbot pushed them aside. He was an old man, and his long beard was white. He faltered when he walked, but he was their spiritual leader and he alone would challenge the demons of the dark.

He flung the door open.

There was a roar of laughter such as had never been heard in the monastery before.

For there, clinging to the bell rope, swinging to and fro, was Ciel, covered in dust and fluff, his fur bristling, his eyes angry. He was starving

and he had been to the refectory and found they had forgotten his plate of food. He could not find any of the holy Fathers, and he knew that food always came when the bell was rung, so he had rung the bell.

He dropped from the rope and led the way to the refectory and a hilarious procession followed him, the cook racing to the kitchen to bring milk and meat, the holy Fathers rejoicing that their pet was found.

Father Guiseppe, who came from Italy, was the cook. He brought meat and he brought milk and he brought goat cheese, knowing that Ciel loved it, and they stood around, forgetting their duties, watching the cat.

He finished his food.

He was cold. Very cold.

He stalked to the kitchen and wailed because his box had vanished. Father Anselm brought it from the cupboard and filled the stone bottle and

Ciel tucked himself down. Father Jerome brought a damp cloth and dusted the dirty fur.

Where could he have been?

Down in the village the people shrugged. The holy Fathers had gone mad, but that was not surprising, seeing the life they led, isolated there on the mountain. It was more than men could endure. It was some weeks before the villagers settled, as they were expecting to hear again the crazy clanging of the angry bells, instead of the soft chimes that marked the passing hours.

They forgot.

The monks did not forget. Father Jerome, going into the cellar for stores, which were kept there in the cool, found the dusty floor in the rarely used far cellar, marked with a cat's frantic paws as he had paced trying desperately to find a way of escape. He must have run down in the dark while they were carrying up the sacks, and gone unnoticed into the further room and been shut in.

That accounted for the mysterious wails that everyone had heard, but that no one admitted to hearing.

Ciel took great care never to venture into the cellars again.

He was treasured as no cat was treasured, becoming old and wise, making life in the remote mountains happier than it could ever have been without his presence.

Father Martin, who loved to draw, painted a picture of a small cat clinging to a thick rope; the picture was hung in one of the corridors, where everyone passed it, and smiled a reminiscent smile of pleasure at the memory.

No one thought to enlighten the villagers and to this day they still wonder and talk about the day when the holy Fathers went mad and the chimes of the bell angered the air, sounding at the wrong time, uttering a devils' carillon that had no tune and no meaning.

THE CAT AND THE SEA

THE MONKS' VOYAGE

ANONYMOUS (8TH CENTURY)

THREE YOUNG Irish monks went on pilgrimage, with great eagerness. They took no food for the voyage but three cakes. "I'll bring the little cat," said one.

Now when they had got among the great waves they said, "In Christ's name, let us throw our oars into the sea, and throw ourselves on the mercy of the Lord."

This was done.

Soon they came with Christ's help to a beautiful island. There was plenty of firewood and water. "Let's build a church in the middle of our island."

This they did.

The little cat went away exploring. It caught them a salmon. It caught them up to three salmon an hour.

"O God," they said, "our pilgrimage is no pilgrimage now. We have brought plenty of food with us; our cat to feed us. It is wrong to eat his catch. We won't eat what he's brought."

So they lived six watches without food, until a message came from Christ that some was on the altar, half a loaf for each man, and a piece of fish.

From A VOYAGE TO LISBON

HENRY FIELDING

THURSDAY, JULY 11TH, 1754. A most tragical incident fell out this day at sea. While the ship was under sail, a kitten, one of four feline inhabitants of the cabin, fell from the window into the water: an alarm was immediately given to the captain, who was then upon deck, and received it with the utmost concern and many bitter oaths. He immediately gave orders to the steersman; the sails were instantly slackened, and all hands employed to recover the poor animal. I was, I own, extremely surprised; less indeed at the captain's extreme tenderness than at his conceiving any possibility of success; for if puss had had nine thousand instead of nine lives, I concluded they had all been lost. The boatswain, however, had more sanguine hopes, for having stripped himself of his jacket, breeches and shirt, he leaped boldly into the water, and to my great astonishment, in a few minutes returned to the ship, bearing the motionless animal in his mouth. The kitten was now exposed to air and sun on the deck, where its life, of which it retained no symptoms, was despaired of by all.

The captain's humanity did not so totally destroy his philosophy as to make him yield himself up to affliction on this melancholy occasion. Having felt his loss like a man, he resolved to shew he could bear it like one; and, having declared he had rather have lost a cask of rum or brandy, betook himself to threshing at backgammon with the Portuguese friar, in which innocent amusement they passed about two-thirds of their time.

The kitten at last recovered, to the great joy of the good captain, but to the great disappointment of some of the sailors, who asserted that the drowning cat was the very surest way of raising a favourable wind.

Wednesday. He even extended his humanity, if I may so call it, to animals, and even his cats and kittens had large shares in his affection. An instance of which we saw this evening, when the cat, which had shewn it could not be drowned, was found suffocated under a feather-bed in the cabin. I will not endeavour to describe his lamentations than barely by saying they were grievous, and seemed to have some mixture of the Irish howl in them.

THE MURDEROUS CAPTAIN

DAVID GREENE

I T WAS told to me by an old seaman as we sat together in the shade of a public park above the Grand Harbour of Valetta in Malta. Below us, and beyond the busy dockyard, the blue Mediterranean looked peaceful and welcoming, but the man was soon recalling less tranquil seas when he had been the mate aboard a Panamanian-registered, Greek-owned, rust-bucket of a cargo vessel with a French master and a largely Asian crew.

They were homeward bound from Melbourne, and had made good time towards the Cape, when the elderly ship's overtaxed main engine finally packed up and they drifted in high seas while the cursing engineers did their best to patch up the damage so that the vessel could limp into Cape Town.

The captain drank heavily and drove his crew hard, especially the second mate, a German called Hansen, against whom he appeared to nurse a deep personal hatred. None of the other sailors ever understood the cause of his spite, since the man, a shy, unsociable individual in his late thirties, worked hard and did his job efficiently.

"Hansen's only friend aboard was Rhaj, the ship's cat," the sailor told me. "And he was the only person who liked the cat, which was a scruffy, spiteful animal. The German fed the cat, allowed it to sleep on his bunk and talked to it for hours on end." It would follow him like a dog wherever he went on the ship.

The engine breakdown made the captain even more short-tempered than usual and most of his anger was vented on the unfortunate second mate. One night he arrived on the bridge well the worse for drink and began to abuse the helmsman for not doing his job properly. The second mate protested and the captain struck him in the face, sending the man spinning against a steel bulkhead. His head struck an angle of metal with savage force, which cracked his skull, killing him instantly.

He was buried at sea the following day. That evening, when the watch changed, the ship's cat appeared on the bridge and stayed staring impassively towards the spot where his friend used to stand on duty. When the time came for the mate to go below, the cat rose and pattered silently away. His strange behaviour quickly attracted the attention of the crew, for according to them, the pattern of his behaviour exactly followed the dead man's daily routine.

He woke at the same time and walked to the washroom and heads, then proceeded to the saloon before making his rounds of the vessel. Before long the seamen concluded that the cat wasn't merely acting out the second mate's daily schedule of activities, he was actually following the ghost of his friend around the vessel. As the rumours spread, the crew, already unnerved by the second mate's violent death, became even more unsettled. Soon the whole ship was filled with dark forebodings.

The captain, who by now seemed to spend more time drunk than sober, ordered his officers to catch the cat and toss him over the side in the hope of calming his sailors down. But no sooner had the order been given than Rhaj vanished from sight. The next time he was seen, two days later, he was curled contently on the dead captain's face.

The man had apparently collapsed onto his bunk while drunk and fallen asleep. Somehow Rhaj had managed to get into the cabin and curl up over the man's mouth and nose, very effectively suffocating him. When the ship docked, the cat walked quietly down the gangway and was never seen again.

"The strange thing was the lock," the seaman who recounted this tale to me concluded. "The captain always locked his cabin door from the inside. It was like that when we found it. They had to break the door open to get in. There *was* a spare key – the skipper kept it in a drawer of his chart table on the bridge. Not many of the crew knew it was there – he liked to have his little secrets, did the old man. But there was one person who, to my certain knowledge, knew exactly where the key was kept. That was the dead second mate, Hansen."

EVERY PORT IN THE WORLD

ANONYMOUS

"EVERY PORT in the world, from Murmansk to South Georgia, from San Diego to Sydney, has been colonised and conquered by the British blotched tabby."

THE CAT AND MURDER

THE LEAST SUCCESSFUL BIRDWATCHERS

ANONYMOUS

IN NOVEMBER 1986 200 birdwatchers from all over Britain gathered in the Scilly Isles to see the arrival of an extremely rare grey-cheeked thrush. During the long wait they discussed the bird's north African habitat, its exquisite colouring and the precise detail of its unusually melodious call.

Peering through binoculars, they saw the priceless bird fly in amidst exclamations regarding its beauty. As soon as it landed on the camp site at St Mary's Garrison, Mrs S. Burrows' cat, Muffin, dashed out, snatched the thrush in its mouth, disappeared into a bush and brought the birdwatching session to a close.

THE RETICENCE OF LADY ANNE

SAKI

EGBERT CAME into the large, dimly lit drawing-room with the air of a man who is not certain whether he is entering a dovecote or a bomb factory, and is prepared for either eventuality. The little domestic quarrel over the luncheon-table had not been fought to a definite finish, and the question was how far Lady Anne was in a mood to renew or forgo hostilities. Her pose in the arm-chair by the tea-table was rather elaborately rigid; in the gloom of a December afternoon Egbert's pince-nez did not materially help him to discern the expression on her face.

By way of breaking whatever ice might be floating on the surface he made a remark about a dim religious light. He or Lady Anne were accustomed to make that remark between 4.30 and 6 on winter and late autumn evenings; it was a part of their married life. There was no recognized rejoinder to it, and Lady Anne made none.

Don Tarquinio lay astretch on the Persian rug, basking in the firelight with superb indifference to the possible ill-humour of Lady Anne. His pedigree was as flawlessly Persian as the rug, and his ruff was coming into the glory of its second winter. The page-boy, who had Renaissance tendencies, had christened him Don Tarquinio. Left to themselves, Egbert and Lady Anne would unfailingly have called him Fluff, but they were not obstinate.

Egbert poured himself out some tea. As the silence gave no sign of breaking on Lady Anne's initiative, he braced himself for another Yermak effort.

"My remark at lunch had a purely academic application," he announced; "you seem to put an unnecessarily personal significance into it."

Lady Anne maintained her defensive barrier of silence. The bullfinch lazily filled in the interval with an air from *Iphigénie en Tauride*. Egbert recognized it immediately, because it was the only air the bullfinch whistled, and he had come to them with the reputation for whistling it. Both Egbert and Lady Anne would have preferred something from *The Yeoman of The Guard*, which was their favourite opera. In matters artistic they had a similarity of taste. They leaned towards the honest and explicit in art, a

99

picture, for instance, that told its own story, with generous assistance from its title. A riderless warhorse with harness in obvious disarray, staggering into a courtyard full of pale swooning women, and marginally noted "Bad News," suggested to their minds a distinct interpretation of some military catastrophe. They could see what it was meant to convey, and explain it to friends of duller intelligence.

The silence continued. As a rule Lady Anne's displeasure became articulate and markedly voluble after four minutes of introductory muteness. Egbert seized the milk-jug and poured some of its contents into Don Tarquinio's saucer; as the saucer was already full to the brim an unsightly overflow was the result. Don Tarquinio looked on with a surprised interest that evanesced into elaborate unconsciousness when he was appealed to by Egbert to come and drink up some of the spilt matter. Don Tarquinio was prepared to play many roles in life, but a vacuum carpet-cleaner was not one of them.

"Don't you think we're being rather foolish?" said Egbert cheerfully.

If Lady Anne thought so she didn't say so.

"I daresay the fault has been partly on my side," continued Egbert, with evaporating cheerfulness. "After all, I'm only human, you know. You seem to forget that I'm only human."

He insisted on the point, as if there had been unfounded suggestions that he was built on Satyr lines, with goat continuations where the human left off.

The bullfinch recommended its air from *Iphigénie en Tauride*. Egbert began to feel depressed. Lady Anne was not drinking her tea. Perhaps she was feeling unwell. But when Lady Anne felt unwell she was not wont to be reticent on the subject. "No one knows what I suffer from indigestion" was one of her favourite statements; but the lack of knowledge can only have been caused by defective listening; the amount of information available on the subject would have supplied material for a monograph.

Evidently Lady Anne was not feeling unwell.

Egbert began to think he was being unreasonably dealt with; naturally he began to make concessions.

"I daresay," he observed, taking as central a position on the hearth-rug as Don Tarquinio could be persuaded to concede him, "I may have been to blame. I am willing, if I can thereby restore things to a happier standpoint, to undertake to lead a better life."

He wondered vaguely how it would be possible. Temptations came to him, in middle age, tentatively and without insistence, like a neglected butcher-boy who asks for a Christmas box in February for no more hopeful reason than that he didn't get one in December. He had no more idea of succumbing to them than he had of purchasing the fish-knives and fur boas that ladies are impelled to sacrifice through the medium of advertisement columns during twelve months of the year. Still, there was something impressive in this unasked-for renunciation of possibly latent enormities.

Lady Anne showed no sign of being impressed.

Egbert looked at her nervously through his glasses. To get the worst of an argument with her was no new experience. To get the worst of a monologue was a humiliating novelty.

"I shall go and dress for dinner," he announced in a voice into which he intended some shade of sternness to creep.

At the door a final access of weakness impelled him to make a further appeal.

"Aren't we being very silly?"

"A fool," was Don Tarquinio's mental comment as the door closed on Egbert's retreat. Then he lifted his velvet forepaws in the air and leapt lightly on to a bookshelf immediately under the bullfinch's cage. It was the first time he had seemed to notice the bird's existence, but he was carrying out a long-formed theory of action with the precision of mature deliberation. The bullfinch, who had fancied himself something of a despot, depressed himself of a sudden into a third of his normal displacement; then he fell to a helpless wing-beating and shrill cheeping. He had cost twenty-seven shillings without the cage, but Lady Anne made no sign of interfering. She had been dead for two hours.

TRAGEDY FOR THREE ACTORS

ROBERT WESTALL

Screaming catastrophe in the yard;
Love, come quick, she's caught a bird;
Starlings diving, going mad
Around Victoria. Black and slim,
petted and pert and mother of three
adorable kittens curled up in a drawer,
Victoria, she looks at me.
(Her mouthful of feathers is moving a claw.)
Grab round her neck, make her release;
deep in her throat the growling comes,
not so much heard as felt through my palms.
Choking's the only way,
thumb across nostrils and tighten her throat,
feeling her tremble.
Knowing me enemy,
she crunches down; so that I feel
through her thin skull-bones
another skull breaking.

The baby starling drops,
blood running ruby by its eye.
Thank God it's dead,
till one leg lifts and lowers
with obscene vitality.
Flinging Victoria into the cupboard
(Soft paws on hard tiles)
I slam the door on her,
go back to the leg still moving
my wife can't touch.
If it were alive I could, she says,
or if it were dead. I pick it up
inside a duster, and take it to the shed
to die in decent privacy.
It would have died more mercifully
in the cat's mouth. The cat
distrusts me now, looking up
from the place where I made her drop it.

MOUSER AND RATTER

GYLES BRANDRETH

Best mouser: Tortoiseshell called Towser, Glenturret Distillery, Crieff, Tayside. Three mice a day. By the time she was 21 in 1984, 23,000 mice.

Best ratter: Female tabby called Minnie. White City Stadium, London. 12,480 rats between 1927 and 1932.

MAHER-SHALAL-HASHBAZ

DOROTHY L. SAYERS

NO LONDONER can ever resist the attraction of a street crowd. Mr Montague Egg, driving up Kingsway, and observing a group of people staring into the branches of one of the slender plane-trees which embellish that thoroughfare, drew up to see what all the excitement was about.

"Poor puss!" cried the bystanders, snapping encouraging fingers. "Poor pussy, then! Kitty, kitty, kitty, come on!"

"Look, baby, look at the pretty pussy!"

"Fetch her a bit of cat's-meat."

"She'll come down when she's tired of it."

"Chuck a stone at her!"

"Now then, what's all this about?"

The slender, shabby child who stood so forlornly holding the empty basket appealed to the policeman.

"Oh, do please send these people away! How *can* he come down, with everybody shouting at him? He's frightened, poor darling."

From among the swaying branches a pair of amber eyes gleamed wrathfully down. The policeman scratched his head.

"Bit of a job, ain't it, missie? However did he come to get up there?"

"The fastening came undone, and he jumped out of the basket just as we were getting off the bus. Oh, please do something!"

Mr Montague Egg, casting his eye over the crowd, perceived on its outskirts a window-cleaner with his ladders upon a truck. He hailed him.

"Fetch that ladder along, sonnie, and we'll soon get him down, if you'll allow me to try, miss. If we leave him to himself, he'll probably stick up there for ages. 'It's hard to reassure, persuade, or charm the customer who once has felt alarm.' Carefully, now. That's the ticket."

"Oh, thank you so much! Oh, do be gentle with him. He does so hate being handled."

"That's all right, miss; don't you worry. Always the gentleman, that's Monty Egg. Kind about the house and clean with children. Up she goes!"

And Mr Egg, clapping his smart trilby upon his head and uttering crooning noises, ascended into the leafage. A loud explosion of spitting sounds and a small shower of twigs floated down to the spectators, and presently Mr Egg followed, rather awkwardly, clutching a reluctant bunch of ginger fur. The girl held out the basket, the four furiously kicking legs were somehow bundled in, a tradesman's lad produced a piece of string, the lid was secured, the window-cleaner was rewarded and removed his ladder, and the crowd dispersed. Mr Egg, winding his pocket-handkerchief about a lacerated wrist, picked the scattered leaves out of his collar and straightened his tie.

"Oh, he's scratched you dreadfully!" lamented the girl, her blue eyes large and tragic.

"Not at all," replied Mr Egg. "Very happy to have been of assistance, I am sure. Can I have the pleasure of driving you anywhere? It'll be pleasanter for him than a bus, and if we pull up the windows he can't jump out, even if he does get the basket open again."

The girl protested, but Mr Egg firmly bustled her into his little saloon and inquired where she wanted to go.

"It's this address," said the girl, pulling a newspaper cutting out of her worn handbag. "Somewhere in Soho, isn't it?"

Mr Egg, with some surprise, read the advertisement:

> **WANTED**: hard-working, capable CAT (either sex), to keep down mice in pleasant villa residence and be companion to middle-aged couple. Ten shillings and good home to suitable applicant. Apply personally to Mr John Doe, La Cigale Bienheureuse, Frith St, W., on Tuesday between 11 and 1 o'clock.

"That's a funny set-out," said Mr Egg, frowning.

"Oh! do you think there's anything wrong with it? Is it just a joke?"

"Well," said Mr Egg, "I can't quite see why anybody wants to pay ten bob for an ordinary cat, can you? I mean, they usually come gratis and f.o.b. from somebody who doesn't like drowning kittens. And I don't quite believe in Mr John Doe; he sounds like what they call a legal fiction."

"Oh, dear!" cried the girl, with tears in the blue eyes. "I do so hope it would be all right. You see, we're so dreadfully hard up, with father out of work, and Maggie – that's my stepmother – says she won't keep Maher-shalal-hashbaz any longer, because he scratches the tablelegs and eats as much as a Christian, bless him! – though he doesn't really – only a little milk and a bit of cat's-meat, and he's a beautiful mouser, only there aren't many mice where we live – and I thought, if I could get him a good home – and ten shillings for some new boots for Dad, he needs them so badly –"

"Oh, well, cheer up," said Mr Egg. "Perhaps they're willing to pay for a full-grown, certified mouser. Or – tell you what – it may be one of these cinema stunts. We'll go and see, anyhow; only I think you'd better let me come with you and interview Mr Doe. I'm quite respectable," he added hastily. "Here's my card. Montague Egg, travelling representative of Plummer & Rose, wines and spirits, Piccadilly. Interviewing customers is my long suit. 'The salesman's job is to get the trade – don't leave the house till the deal is made' – that's Monty's motto."

"My name's Jean Maitland, and Dad's in the commercial line himself – at least, he was till he got bronchitis last winter, and now he isn't strong enough to go on the road."

"Bad luck!" said Monty sympathetically, as he turned down High

Holborn. He liked this child of sixteen or so, and registered a vow that "something should be done about it".

It seemed as though there were other people who thought ten shillings good payment for a cat. The pavement before the grubby little Soho restaurant was thick with cat-owners, some carrying baskets, some clutching their animals in their arms. The air resounded with the mournful cries of the prisoners.

"Some competition," said Monty. "Well, anyhow, the post doesn't seem to be filled yet. Hang on to me, and we'll try what we can do."

They waited for some time. It seemed that the applicants were being passed out through a back entrance, for, though many went in, none returned. Eventually they secured a place in the queue going up a dingy staircase, and, after a further eternity, found themselves facing a dark and discouraging door. Presently this was opened by a stout and pursy-faced man, with very sharp little eyes, who said briskly: "Next, please!" and they walked in.

"Mr John Doe?" said Monty.

"Yes. Brought your cat? Oh, the young lady's cat. I see. Sit down, please. Name and address, miss?"

The girl gave an address south of the Thames, and the man made a note of it, "in case," he explained, "the chosen candidate should prove unsuitable, and I might want to write to you again. Now, let us see the cat."

The basket was opened, and a ginger head emerged resentfully.

"Oh, yes. Fine specimen. Poor pussy, then. He doesn't seem very friendly."

"He's frightened by the journey, but he's a darling when he once knows you, and a splendid mouser. And so clean."

"That's important. Must have him clean. And he must work for his living, you know."

"Oh, he will. He can tackle rats or anything. We call him Maher-shalal-hashbaz, because he 'makes haste to the spoil'. But he answers to Mash, don't you, darling?"

"I see. Well, he seems to be in good condition. No fleas? No diseases? My wife is very particular."

"Oh, no. He's a splendid healthy cat. Fleas, indeed!"

"No offence, but I must be particular, because we shall make a great pet of him. I don't care much for his colour. Ten shillings is a high price to pay for a ginger one. I don't know whether – "

"Come, come," said Monty. "Nothing was said in your advertisement about colour. This lady has come a long way to bring you the cat, and you can't expect her to take less than she's offered. You'll never get a better cat than this; everyone knows that the ginger ones are the best mousers – they've got more go in them. And look at his handsome white shirt-front. It *shows* you how beautifully clean he is. And think of the advantage – you can see him – you and your good lady won't go tripping over him in a dark corner, same as you do with these black and tabby ones. As a matter of fact, we ought to charge extra for such a handsome colour as this. They're much rarer and more high-class than the ordinary cat."

"There's something in that," admitted Mr Doe. "Well, look here, Miss Maitland. Suppose you bring Maher – what you said – out to our place this evening, and if my wife likes him we will keep him. Here's the address. And you must come at six precisely, please, as we shall be going out later."

Monty looked at the address, which was at the northern extremity of the Edgware-Morden Tube.

"It's a very long way to come on the chance," he said resolutely. "You will have to pay Miss Maitland's expenses."

"Oh, certainly," said Mr Doe. "That's only fair. Here is half a crown. You can return me the change this evening. Very well, thank you. Your cat will have a really happy home if he comes to us. Put him back in his basket now. The other way out, please. Mind the step. *Good* morning."

Mr Egg and his new friend, stumbling down an excessively confined and stuffy back staircase into a malodorous by-street, looked at one another.

"He seemed rather an abrupt sort of person," said Miss Maitland. "I do *hope* he'll be kind to Maher-shalal-hashbaz. You were *marvellous* about the gingeriness – I thought he was going to be stuffy about that. My angel Mash! how *anybody* could object to his beautiful colour!"

"Um!" said Mr Egg. "Well, Mr Doe may be O.K., but I shall believe in his ten shillings when I see it. And, in any case, you're not going to his house alone. I shall call for you in the car at five o'clock."

"But, Mr Egg – I can't allow you! Besides, you've taken half a crown off him for my fare."

"That's only business," said Mr Egg. "Five o'clock sharp I shall be there."

"Well, come at four, and let us give you a cup of tea, anyway. That's the least we can do."

"Pleased, I'm sure," said Mr Egg.

The house occupied by Mr John Doe was a new detached villa standing solitary at the extreme end of a new and unmade suburban road. It was Mrs Doe who answered the bell – a small, frightened-looking woman with watery eyes and a nervous habit of plucking at her pale lips with her fingers. Maher-shalal-hashbaz was released from his basket in the sitting-room, where Mr Doe was reclining in an armchair, reading the evening paper. The cat sniffed suspiciously at him, but softened to Mrs Doe's timid advances so far as to allow his ears to be tickled.

"Well, my dear," said Mr Doe, "will he do? You don't object to the colour, eh?"

"Oh, no. He's a beautiful cat. I like him very much."

"Right. Then we'll take him. Here you are, Miss Maitland. Ten shillings. Please sign this receipt. Thanks. Never mind about the change from the half-crown. There you are, my dear; you've got your cat, and I hope we shall see no more of those mice. Now" – he glanced at his watch – "I'm afraid you must say good-bye to your pet quickly, Miss Maitland; we've got to get off. He'll be quite safe with us."

Monty strolled out with gentlemanly reticence into the hall while the last words were said. It was, no doubt, the same gentlemanly feeling which led him to move away from the sitting-room door towards the back part of the house; but he had only waited a very few minutes when Jean Maitland came out, sniffing valiantly into a small handkerchief, and followed by Mrs Doe.

"You're fond of your cat, aren't you, my dear? I do hope you don't feel too –"

"There, there, Flossie," said her husband, appearing suddenly at her shoulders, "Miss Maitland knows he'll be well looked after." He showed them out, and shut the door quickly upon them.

"If you *don't* feel happy about it," said Mr Egg uneasily, "we'll have him back in two twos."

"No, it's all right," said Jean. "If you don't mind, let's get in at once and drive away – rather fast."

As they lurched over the uneven road, Mr Egg saw a lad coming down it. In one hand he carried a basket. He was whistling loudly.

"Look!" said Monty. "One of our hated rivals. We've got in ahead of him, anyhow. 'The salesman first upon the field gets the bargain signed and sealed.' Damn it!" he added to himself, as he pressed down the accelerator, "I *hope* it's O.K. I wonder."

Although Mr Egg had worked energetically to get Maher-shalal-hashbaz settled in the world, he was not easy in his mind. The matter preyed upon his spirits to such an extent that, finding himself back in London on the following Saturday week, he made an expedition south of the Thames to make inquiries. And when the Maitlands' door was opened by Jean, there by her side, arching his back and brandishing his tail, was Maher-shalal-hashbaz.

"Yes," said the girl, "he found his way back, the clever darling! Just a week ago today – and he was dreadfully thin and draggled – how he did it, I can't think. But we simply couldn't send him away again, could we, Maggie?"

"No," said Mrs Maitland. "I don't like the cat, and never did, but there! I suppose even cats have their feelings. But it's an awkward thing about the money."

"Yes," said Jean. "You see, when he got back and we decided to keep him, I wrote to Mr Doe and explained, and sent him a postal order for the ten shillings. And this morning the letter came back from the Post Office, marked 'Not Known'. So we don't know what to do about it."

"I never did believe in Mr John Doe," said Monty. "If you ask me, Miss Maitland, he was no good, and I shouldn't bother any more about him."

But the girl was not satisfied, and presently the obliging Mr Egg found himself driving out northwards in search of the mysterious Mr Doe, carrying the postal order with him.

The door of the villa was opened by a neatly dressed, elderly woman whom he had never seen before. Mr Egg inquired for Mr John Doe.

"He doesn't live here. Never heard of him."

Monty explained that he wanted the gentleman who had purchased the cat.

"Cat?" said the woman. Her face changed. "Step inside, will you? George!" she called to somebody inside the house, "here's a gentleman called about a cat. Perhaps you'd like to –" The rest of the sentence was whispered into the ear of a man who emerged from the sitting-room, and who appeared to be, and was in fact, her husband.

George looked Mr Egg carefully up and down. "I don't know nobody here called Doe," said he; "but if it's the late tenant you're wanting, they've left. Packed and went off in a hurry the day after the old gentleman was buried. I'm the caretaker for the landlord. And if you've missed a cat, maybe you'd like to come and have a look out here."

He led the way through the house and out at the back door into the garden. In the middle of one of the flower-beds was a large hole, like an irregularly shaped and shallow grave. A spade stood upright in the mould. And laid in two lugubrious rows upon the lawn were the corpses of some very dead cats. At a hasty estimate, Mr Egg reckoned that there must be close on fifty of them.

"If any of these is yours," said George, "you're welcome to it. But they ain't in what you might call good condition."

"Good Lord!" said Mr Egg, appalled, and thought with pleasure of Maher-shalal-hashbaz, tail erect, welcoming him on the Maitlands' threshold. "Come back and tell me about this. It's – it's unbelievable!"

It turned out that the name of the late tenants had been Proctor. The family consisted of an old Mr Proctor, an invalid, to whom the house belonged, and his married nephew and the nephew's wife.

"They didn't have no servant sleeping in. Old Mrs Crabbe used to do for them, coming in daily, and she always told me that the old gentleman couldn't abide cats. They made him ill like – I've known folks like that afore. And, of course, they had to be careful, him being so frail and his heart so bad he might have popped off any minute. What it seemed to us when I found all them cats buried, like, was as how maybe young Proctor had killed them to prevent the old gentleman seeing 'em and getting a shock. But the queer thing is that all them cats looks to have been killed about the same time and not so long ago, neither."

Mr Egg remembered the advertisement, and the false name, and the applicants passed out by a different door, so that none of them could possibly tell how many cats had been bought and paid for. And he remembered also the careful injunction to bring the cat at six o'clock precisely, and the whistling lad with the basket who had appeared on the scene about a quarter of an hour after them. He remembered another thing – a faint miauling noise that had struck upon his ear as he stood in the hall while Jean was saying good-bye to Maher-shalal-hashbaz, and the worried look on Mrs Proctor's face when she had asked if Jean was fond of her pet. It looked as though Mr Proctor junior had been collecting cats for some rather sinister purpose. Collecting them from every quarter of London. From quarters as far apart as possible – or why so much care to take down names and addresses?

. "What did the old gentleman die of?" he asked.

"Well," said Mrs George, "it was just heart-failure, or so the doctor said. Last Tuesday week he passed away in the night, poor soul, and Mrs Crabbe that laid him out said he had a dreadful look of horror on his poor face, but the doctor said that wasn't anything out of the way, not with his disease. But what the doctor didn't see, being too busy to come round, was them terrible scratches on his face and arms. Must have regular clawed himself in his agony – oh, dear, oh, dear! But there! Anybody knew as he might go off at any time like the blowing out of a candle."

"I know that, Sally," said her husband, "but what about them scratches on the bedroom door? Don't tell me he did that, too. Or, if he did, why didn't somebody hear him and come along to help him? It's all very well for Mr Timbs – that's the landlord – to say as tramps must have got into the house after the Proctors left, and put us in here to look after the place, but why should tramps go for to do a useless bit of damage like that?"

"A 'eartless lot, them Proctors, that's what I say," said Mrs George. "A-snoring away, most likely, and leaving their uncle to die by himself. And wasn't the lawyer upset about it, neither! Coming along in the morning to make the old gentleman's will, and him passed away so sudden. And seeing they came in for all his money after all, you'd think they might have given him a better funeral. Mean, I call it – not a flower, hardly – only one half-guinea wreath – and no oak – only elm and a shabby lot of handles. Such trash! You'd think they'd be ashamed."

Mr Egg was silent. He was not a man of strong imagination, but he saw a very horrible picture in his mind. He saw an old, sick man asleep, and hands that quietly opened the bedroom door, and dragged in, one after the other, sacks that moved and squirmed and mewed. He saw the sacks left open on

the floor, and the door being softly shut and locked on the outside. And then, in the dim glow of the night-light, he saw shadowy shapes that leapt and flitted about the room – black and tabby and ginger – up and down, prowling on noiseless feet, thudding on velvet paws from tables and chairs. And then, plump up on the bed – a great ginger cat with amber eyes – and the sleeper waking with a cry – and after that a nightmare of terror and disgust behind the locked and remorseless door. A very old, sick man, stumbling and gasping for breath, striking out at the shadowy horrors that pursued and fled him – and the last tearing pain at the heart when merciful death overtook him. Then, nothing but a mewing of cats and a scratching at the door, and outside, the listener, with his ear bent to the keyhole.

Mr Egg passed his handkerchief over his forehead; he did not like his thoughts. But he had to go on, and see the murderer sliding through the door in the morning – hurrying to collect his innocent accomplices before Mrs Crabbe should come – knowing that it must be done quickly and the corpse made decent – and that when people came to the house there must be no mysterious miaulings to surprise them. To set the cats free would not be enough – they might hang about the house. No; the water-butt and then the grave in the garden. But Maher-shalal-hashbaz – noble Maher-shalal-hashbaz had fought for his life. He was not going to be drowned in any water-butts. He had kicked himself loose ("and I hope," thought Mr Egg, "he scratched him all to blazes"), and he had toiled his way home across London. If only Maher-shalal-hashbaz could tell what he knew! But Monty Egg knew something, and he could tell.

"And I *will* tell, what's more," said Monty Egg to himself, as he wrote down the name and address of Mr Proctor's solicitor. He supposed it must be murder to terrify an old man to death; he was not sure, but he meant to find out. He cast about in his mind for a consoling motto from the *Salesman's Handbook*, but, for the first time in his life, could find nothing that really fitted the case.

"I seem to have stepped regularly out of my line," he thought sadly; "but still, as a citizen – "

And then he smiled, recollecting the first and last aphorism in his favourite book:

> *To serve the Public is the aim*
> *Of every salesman worth the name.*

THE CAT AND WAR

THE TRAPEZE ARTISTE

DAVID GREENE

O N ONE occasion, a cat had been shut up in a house with her kittens, while the owners were away at work. Sensing imminent danger, she desperately searched the house for a way of escape and finally discovered a partially open back bedroom window. The drop into the garden was too great a risk, and there was no convenient drainpipe or nearby tree to use as a ladder. Then the resourceful cat noticed that a telephone line connected up to the house close to the window, and this thin cable became her lifeline. Lifting the kittens out of their basket in the kitchen, she carried them upstairs one by one, and then onto the window ledge. Next, she leaped nimbly onto the line and balanced there, a protesting kitten held firmly by the scruff of the neck, before stalking, as calmly and confidently as any high-wire artiste, to the telegraph pole. From there she scrambled down into the garden and placed the kitten on an old piece of sacking in the garden shed. With that rescue mission concluded she then retraced her precarious route into the house to carry another of her young out of the house. Soon after the last kitten had been transported safely, a bomb fell nearby and the house was badly damaged by the blast. The kitchen in which the cat and her kittens had been lying was showered with a fusillade of jagged glass. If the cat had not somehow foreseen the danger, it seems certain that all would have been seriously, perhaps fatally, injured.

CLEVER CAT

From "THE CAT"
THE OFFICIAL JOURNAL OF THE CATS PROTECTION LEAGUE

I N THE early days of the war, single German bombers used to fly over London, some to drop bombs, some flying over to other cities. Every time a German plane went over, my cat went under his chosen "air raid shelter" – the electric cooker! If a British plane passed overhead, he took no notice at all. How did he know the difference? Indeed, he used to hear the German planes at least half a minute before I did.

REPORT ON A FRIENDSHIP

GRACE FLANDRAU

A FTER DIGGING among rubble for several hours he unearthed a very frightened and bedraggled tabby and persuaded her to drink a saucer of milk. Then he tried to coax her into a basket, but puss would not leave the debris. She even tried to re-enter the hole through which he had just pulled her, so the inspector made further excavations and found a little black dog, badly wounded, crouching there in the bombhole. It was gently lifted out and tended, to the evident satisfaction of the cat, and later the rescue workers found the two animals were the inseparable pets of a family who had been killed, save for one member, on the night of the raid . . .

FEARS FOR MY CAT

From "THE CAT"
THE OFFICIAL JOURNAL OF THE CATS PROTECTION LEAGUE

THAT DREADFUL question of what to do in a sudden invasion! I am haunted by the thought of frightened semi-hysterical cat-owners trying to put an end to their cats in a few panicky minutes. I am assured by my local authorities that my first duty is to "stay put" in case of an alarm. Therefore I need not fear being hurriedly turned out of my house. I live in a semi-rural place, with plenty of trees and bushes about and a real wood about two minutes cat run away. When strangers, noisy ones especially, like plumbers, come to the house, my cat departs to some bush or other, and duly returns when the work is over. He is nervous but self-possessed. At the first alarm I shall open all the doors and windows and trust to his wonderful instincts. If the enemy reaches the house I am certain he will keep away, and as certain he will come back when they have gone. Should I be killed in the meantime, the neighbours within reach, the police, the veterinary surgeon, the usual tradesmen, all have his description, and injunctions to look out for him. We shall not all be killed, and he will be taken in and sent to a prearranged place where he will be put to sleep. If I survive, he will rejoin me when the noise of the war has passed elsewhere.

WARTIME CATS

From "THE CAT"
THE OFFICIAL JOURNAL OF THE CATS PROTECTION LEAGUE

TWO DAYS before the close of 1941, the Minister of Food announced that cats "engaged in work of national importance" were to receive an allowance of powdered milk, drawn from supplies damaged in handling and so unfit for human consumption. "Cats so privileged," commented the Daily Telegraph, "must be engaged in keeping down mice and rats in warehouses in which at least 250 tons of food or animal feeding stuffs are stored."

WAR CAT

DOROTHY L. SAYERS

I am sorry, my little cat, I am sorry —
if I had it, you should have it;
but there is a war on.

No, there are no table-scraps;
there was only an omelette
made from dehydrated eggs,
and baked apples to follow, and we finished it all.
The butcher has no lights,
the fishmonger has no cod's heads
there is nothing for you
but cat-biscuit
and those remnants of yesterday's ham;
you must do your best with it.

Round and pathetic eyes,
baby mouth opened in a reproachful cry,
how can I explain to you?
I know, I know;
"Mistress, it is not nice;
the ham is very salt
and the cat-biscuit very dull,
I sniffed at it, and the smell was not enticing.
Do you not love me any more?
Mistress, I do my best for the war-effort;
I killed four mice last week,
yesterday I caught a young stoat.
You stroked and praised me,
you called me a clever cat.

"What have I done to offend you?
I am industrious, I earn my keep;
I am not like the parrot, who sits there
using bad language and devouring
parrot-seed at eight-and-sixpence a pound
without working for it."

"If you will not pay me my wages
there is no justice;
if you have ceased to love me
there is no charity.

"See, now, I rub myself against your legs
to express my devotion,
which is not altered by any unkindness.
My little heart is contracted
because your goodwill is withdrawn from me;
my ribs are rubbing together
for lack of food,
but indeed I cannot eat this
my soul revolts at the sight of it.
I have tried, believe me,
but it was like ashes in my mouth.
If your favour is departed
and your bowels of compassion are shut up,
then all that is left me
is to sit in a draught on the stone floor and look miserable
till I die of starvation
and a broken heart."

Cat with the innocent face,
what can I say?
Everything is very hard on everybody.
If you were a little Greek cat,
or a little Polish cat,
there would be nothing for you at all,
not even cat-food:
indeed, you would be lucky
if you were not eaten yourself.
Think if you were a little Russian cat
prowling among the cinders of a deserted city!
Consider that pains and labour
and the valour of merchant-seamen and fishermen
have gone even to the making of this biscuit
which smells so unappetizing.
Alas! there is no language
in which I can tell you these things.

Well, well!
If you will not be comforted
we will put the contents of your saucer
into the chicken-bowl – there!
all gone! nasty old cat-food –
The hens, I dare say,
will be grateful for it.

Wait only a little
and I will go to the butcher
and see if by any chance
he can produce some fragments of the insides of something.

Only stop crying
and staring in that unbearable manner –
as soon as I have put on my hat
we will try to do something about it.

My hat is on,
I have put on my shoes,
I have taken my shopping basket –
What are you doing on the table?

The chicken-bowl is licked clean;
there is nothing left in it at all.
Cat,
hell-cat, Hitler-cat, human,
all-too-human cat,
cat corrupt, infected,
instinct with original sin,
cat of a fallen and perverse creation,
hypocrite with the innocent and limpid eyes –
is nothing desirable
till somebody else desires it?

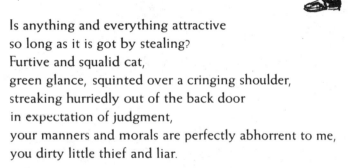

Is anything and everything attractive
so long as it is got by stealing?
Furtive and squalid cat,
green glance, squinted over a cringing shoulder,
streaking hurriedly out of the back door
in expectation of judgment,
your manners and morals are perfectly abhorrent to me,
you dirty little thief and liar.

Nevertheless,
although you have made a fool of me,
yet, bearing in mind your pretty wheedling ways
(not to mention the four mice and the immature stoat),
and having put on my hat to go to the butcher's,
I may as well go.

THE FAT CAT

Q. PATRICK

THE MARINES found her when they finally captured the old mission house at Fufa. After two days of relentless pounding, they hadn't expected to find anything alive there – least of all a fat cat.

And she was a very fat cat, sandy as a Scotchman, with enormous agate eyes and a fat amiable face. She sat there on the mat – or rather what was left of the mat – in front of what had been the mission porch, licking her paws as placidly as if the shell-blasted jungle were a summer lawn in New Jersey.

One of the men, remembering his childhood primer, quoted: "The fat cat sat on the mat."

The other men laughed, not that the remark was really funny, but laughter broke the tension and expressed their relief at having at last reached their objective, after two days of bitter fighting.

The fat cat, still sitting on the mat, smiled at them, as if to show she didn't mind the joke being on her. Then she saw Corporal Randy Jones, and for some reason known only to herself ran toward him as though he was her long-lost master. With a refrigerator purr, she weaved in and out of his muddy legs.

Everyone laughed again as Randy picked her up and pushed his ugly face against the sleek fur. It was funny to see any living thing show a preference for the dour, solitary Randy.

A sergeant flicked his fingers. "Kitty, come here. We'll make you B Company mascot."

But the cat, perched on Randy's shoulder like a queen on her throne, merely smiled down majestically as much as to say: "You can be my subjects if you like. But this is my man – my royal consort."

And never for a second did she swerve from her devotion. She lived with Randy, slept with him, ate only food provided by him. Almost every man in

122

Co. B tried to seduce her with caresses and morsels of canned ration, but all advances were met with a yawn of contempt.

For Randy this new love was ecstasy. He guarded her with the possessive tenderness of a mother. He combed her fur sleek, he almost starved himself to maintain her fatness. And all the time there was a strange wonder in him. The homeliest and ungainliest of ten in a West Virginia mining family, he had never before aroused affection in man or woman. No one had counted for him until the fat cat.

Randy's felicity, however, was short-lived. In a few days B Company was selected to carry out a flanking movement to surprise and possibly capture the enemy's headquarters, known to be twenty miles away through dense, sniper-infested jungle. The going would be rugged. Each man would carry his own supply of food and water, and sleep in foxholes with no support from the base.

The C. O. was definite about the fat cat: the stricken Randy was informed that the presence of a cat would seriously endanger the safety of the whole company. If it were seen following him, it would be shot on sight. Just before their scheduled departure, Randy carried the fat cat over to the mess of Co. H, where she was enthusiastically received by an equally fat cook. Randy could not bring himself to look back at the reproachful stare which he knew would be in the cat's agate eyes.

But all through that first day of perilous jungle travel, the thought of the cat's stare haunted him, and he was prey to all the heartache of parting; in leaving the cat, he had left behind wife, mother and child.

Darkness, like an immense black parachute, had descended hours ago on the jungle, when Randy was awakened from exhausted sleep. Something soft and warm was brushing his cheek; and his foxhole resounded to a symphony of purring. He stretched out an incredulous hand, but this was no dream. Real and solid, the cat was curled in a contended ball at his shoulder.

His first rush of pleasure was chilled as he remembered his C. O.'s words. The cat, spurning the blandishments of H Co.'s cuisine, had followed him through miles of treacherous jungle only to face death the moment daylight revealed her presence. Randy was in an agony of uncertainty. To carry her back to the base would be desertion. To beat and drive her away was beyond the power of his simple nature.

The cat nuzzled his face again and breathed a mournful meow. She was hungry, of course, after her desperate trek. Suddenly Randy saw what he

must do. If he could bring himself not to feed her, hunger would surely drive her back to the sanctuary of the cook.

She meowed again. He shushed her and gave her a half-hearted slap. "Ain't got nothing for you, honey. Scram. Go home. Scat!"

To his mingled pleasure and disappointment, she leaped silently out of the foxhole. When morning came there was no sign of her.

As B Company inched its furtive advance through the dense under-growth, Randy felt the visit from the cat must have been a dream. But on the third night it came again. It brushed against his cheek and daintily took his ear in its teeth. When it meowed, the sound was still soft and cautious, but held a pitiful quaver of beseechment which cut through Randy like a Jap bayonet.

On its first visit, Randy had not seen the cat, but tonight some impulse made him reach for his flashlight. Holding it carefully downward, he turned it on. What he saw was the ultimate ordeal. The fat cat was fat no longer. Her body sagged, her sleek fur was matted and mud-stained, her paws torn and bloody. But it was the eyes, blinking up at him, that were the worst. There was no hint of reproach in them, only an expression of infinite trust and pleading.

Forgetting everything but those eyes, Randy tugged out one of his few remaining cans of ration. At sight of it, the cat weakly licked its lips. Randy moved to open the can. Then the realization that he would be signing the cat's death warrant surged over him. And, because the pent-up emotion in him had to have some outlet, it turned into unreasoning anger against this animal whose suffering had become more than he could bear. "Skat," he hissed. But the cat did not move.

He lashed out at her with the heavy flashlight. For a second she lay motionless under the blow. Then with a little moan she fled.

The next night she did not come back and Randy did not sleep.

On the fifth day they reached really dangerous territory. Randy and another marine, Joe, were sent forward to scout for the Jap command headquarters. Suddenly, weaving through the jungle, they came upon it.

A profound silence hung over the glade, with its two hastily erected shacks. Peering through dense foliage, they saw traces of recent evacuation – waste paper scattered on the grass, a pile of fresh garbage, a Jap army shirt flapping on a tree. Outside one of the shacks, under an awning, stretched a rough table strewn with the remains of a meal. "They must have got wind of us and scrammed," breathed Joe.

Randy edged forward – then froze as something stirred in the long grasses near the door of the first shack. As he watched, the once fat cat hobbled out into the sunlight.

A sense of heightened danger warred with Randy's pride that she had not abandoned him. Stiff with suspense, he watched it disappear into the shack. Soon it padded out.

"No Japs," said Joe. "That cat'd have raised 'em sure as shooting."

He started boldly into the glade. "Hey, Randy, there's a whole chicken on that table. Chicken's going to taste good after K ration."

He broke off, for the cat had seen the chicken too, and with pitiful clumsiness had leaped onto the table. With an angry yell Joe stooped for a rock and threw it.

Indignation blazed in Randy. He'd starved and spurned the cat, and yet she'd followed him with blind devotion. The chicken, surely, should be her reward. In his slow, simple mind it seemed the most important thing in the world for his beloved to have her fair share of the booty.

The cat, seeing the rock coming, jumped off the table just in time, for the rock struck the chicken squarely, knocking it off its plate.

Randy leaped into the clearing. As he did so, a deafening explosion made him drop to the ground. A few seconds later, when he raised himself, there was no table, no shack, nothing but blazing wreckage of wood.

Dazedly he heard Joe's voice: "Booby trap under that chicken. Gee, if that cat hadn't jumped for it, I wouldn't have hurled the rock; we'd have grabbed it ourselves – and we'd be in heaven now." His voice dropped to an awed whisper. "That cat. I guess it's blown to hell . . . But it saved our lives." Randy couldn't speak. There was a constriction in his throat. He lay there, feeling more desolate than he'd ever felt in his life before.

Then from behind him came a contented purr.

He spun round. Freakishly, the explosion had hurled a crude rush mat out of the shack. It had come to rest on the grass behind him.

And, seated serenely on the mat, the cat was smiling at him.

EAST DODDINGHAM DINAH

ROBERT WESTALL

E AST DODDINGHAM Dinah was never a ghost; at least till the end.

She was a living cat; yet as near a ghost as a living cat can be. Long white fur and pale blue eyes. When she let you pick her up (which wasn't often) you'd realise half of her was fur. Only deep inside that luxurious fur you'd feel thin bones and thinner muscles, frail as wire. She hardly weighed a thing. All soul, she was; a loving soul looking out of huge dark unfathomable eyes, set in a head like a beautiful white skull. I never saw a cat that could jump like her; she could almost fly, like the frail thin aeroplanes she loved.

East Doddingham? East Doddingham was a World War II bomber airfield, set in the bleak wastes of Lincolnshire. The evening Dinah arrived, it was under a shroud of snow and thin fog, so it's no puzzle why the ground-crews never saw her.

She was looking for warmth, like the rest of us. But she didn't, like any ordinary cat, make for the glowing stoves of the Nissen huts, or the greasy delights of the cook-house. She must have climbed up the ladder into B-Baker, on the dispersal pad.

She must have made herself snug in the best place; the rest bed that's halfway down the tail, towards the rear gun turret. Rest bed they called it; that was a laugh. Who can rest on a bombing mission? The rest bed is where we put the dying and the dead; the snug-looking red blankets don't show the blood.

Anyway, the neatly folded piles of blankets were good enough for Dinah. She must have buried herself in them; nobody noticed her till after take-off.

If we'd obeyed orders, she'd have soon been dead. We were supposed to fly at 26,000 feet where the Jerry night fighters couldn't get at us so easily.

At 26,000 feet there's so little air her lungs would have burst. But I followed the gospel according to Mickey Martin. 7,000 feet, where the light anti-aircraft guns are out of range, and the big ones can't draw a bead on you quick enough. I'd followed the gospel according to Mickey Martin for a year; Mickey was still alive, and so was I.

But it's still bitterly cold at 7,000, and it must have been the cold that drove her out. She made for the nearest human she could smell; who was Luke Goodman our rear gunner. Luke had left his armoured doors a touch open, and she slipped through and on to his lap as if he was sitting by his own fireside. How can she have known that, of all of us, Luke was the one who was mad about cats?

Anyway, Luke had a lot to offer her, besides his lap. He'd shoved the nozzle of the hot-air hose down his right flying boot, so the air would flow up nicely round his crotch. So Dinah got the full benefit. And of course he was starting to nibble nervously at his huge greasy pack of corned beef sandwiches . . . And in return she rubbed her white head against his face, and kept him nicely insulated where it mattered most. The pair of them must have been in Heaven. Until Luke hit his first problem.

We were over the North Sea by that time; time to test his guns. He put it off as long as he could, scared the din would frighten her away. But in the end, those twin Brownings are all that stands between a tail-end-Charlie and a nasty end splattered all over the inside of his turret. So he fired them.

She didn't flinch an inch; only watched the lines of red tracer flying away behind with an interested lift of her head. It was then he realised that, being white with blue eyes, she was stone deaf, of course. How else could she have borne the endless deafening roar of the engines without going mad?

Anyway, quite oblivious of all this, I made landfall on the enemy coast; picked up the island of Texel, and headed in over the Zuyder Zee. Not much flak that way in, except for a few useless flak ships. But Jerry put up quite a pretty display as we passed between Arnhem and Nijmegen. Luke told me afterwards that Dinah was fascinated, her head darting this way and that, following every flash and line of tracer. She didn't shiver; she sort of quivered with excitement, sometimes dabbing out a paw as if to catch the red and yellow slow-floating balls.

Frankly, when he told me afterwards, I broke out in a cold sweat . . . If he was so busy playing with that damned cat, how could he possibly have his eyes skinned for night fighters? On the other hand, she was at least keeping him awake. For the danger is not the flak, not at our height. But the quiet

127

bits between, when you seem to be flying alone through an empty moonlit
sky, and the war might be on another planet. That's when rear gunners
actually fall asleep through cold and loneliness and boredom, and the
weariness after terror. As skipper, I had to keep on yakking at them, down
the intercom, nagging them like a wife, asking if their nose is running or
their feet are freezing. Anything to keep them awake. For it's in the peace
and moonlit quiet that the night fighters come. Creeping in beneath your
belly till they're only fifteen metres away, and they can't possibly miss with
their fixed upward-pointing cannons.

Anyway, in the quiet bit before we hit the Ruhr, or Happy Valley as we
called it, Luke said he was wide awake, and so was Dinah, just purring like a
little engine. He couldn't hear her, of course, but he could feel her throat
vibrating against his knee.

Then suddenly, she seemed to see something he couldn't. She tensed,
flicked her head from side to side, as if to get a better view, then dabbed out
swift as lightning with her right paw, against the perspex of the turret
window.

Luke looked where she'd dabbed; but he couldn't see a bloody thing.

She tensed and dabbed out again. And still he couldn't see anything. He
began to wonder if it wasn't one of those tiny black flies you get in
Lincolnshire, the ones cats chase when you think they're chasing nothing.

And then she dabbed again; and he saw it. Even smaller than a fly on the
perspex. A grey shape against the clouds below that could only be a Jerry.
Out of range, but hoping to creep up beneath us. Luke was the first to admit
that, without Dinah, he'd never have seen it. But now he had seen it, he had
the edge; he felt like God, with Dinah on his knee. Invincible.

128

So he didn't warn me, like he should have done. He just eased his turret round ever so slowly, so that Jerry wouldn't spot that he'd been lumbered. Got Jerry in his ring-sight and watched him grow.

Luke said the Jerry was one of the best, a real craftsman. Took advantage of every bit of cloud to climb, get a bit nearer. Soon Luke could see he was an ME 110, with more radar antennae bristling on its nose than a cat's got whiskers. No front guns to worry about, then: only the fixed upward-pointing cannons behind the cockpit that Jerry couldn't use until he was directly under our belly . . .

Luke waited; waited until he could see the black mottle on its grey wings; waited until he could almost read its serial number, till he could see the white face of the pilot looking upwards. Then he gave it a five-second burst, right into the cockpit. He said the cockpit flew apart in a shower of silver rain; but the thing went on flying steadily beneath us. Perhaps the pilot was already dead. But he gave it another five-second burst into the right engine, and the fire grew . . .

I nearly had a heart attack. Luke screaming, "I've got him, skipper, I've *got* him." And suddenly this Jerry in flames appeared directly underneath my nose, so I had to throw the crate upwards and to port, to avoid going with it, when it blew up . . .

I can tell you, the bomb run over Dusseldorf was an anti-climax after that. And the run home was like a party. Because it's not often that a rear gunner gets a night fighter in our lot. I mean, imagine standing on a railway-station platform at night, with kids throwing burning fireworks at you, and a train comes through at a hundred miles an hour and you've got to hit the fat man sitting in the third compartment of the fourth carriage, with your air pistol . . . that's what it's like being a rear gunner. We only got a Jerry once before; in the early days of 1940, a bemused waist gunner in a Wimpey, in the hell over Berlin, saw a Messerschmidt 109, without radar, without a clue, poor sod, sail past his gun at less than a hundred yards range, overtaking a bomber he never even saw. The gunner was so amazed he almost missed the shot. But not quite. The Jerry went down without ever knowing what hit him. But that was the only other time we got one.

But now, my lot thought we were the greatest; thought we were invincible. I was in a cold sweat all the way home, trying to get them to go on keeping a close lookout.

But it wasn't till we crossed the Dutch coast that Luke said he had a cat sitting on his knee.

"Poor sod," said Hoppy the wireless op, over the intercom. "Greatness hath made him mad." Hoppy did a year at Oxford, before he volunteered to be a coconut shy at 26,000 feet over the Ruhr. He hoped to return to complete a degree in English Literature. He may yet make it, if he can find a way to write, with no hands to speak of . . .

There were lots of other witty cracks, catcalls and jeers. But Luke insisted he had a white cat sitting on his knee. And at 7,000 feet, no way could he be goofy through lack of oxygen. So I sent Mike the flight engineer to go and see. Anything goes wrong, I send the flight engineer to go and see; if he's still alive.

Mike poked his head through Luke's armoured doors.

"Gotta cat all right," he reported back.

"What's it doing?"

"Eating sandwiches . . . "

There never was a cat like Dinah for eating. When she finished Luke's she walked forward and scrounged off Hoppy and Bob the navigator, who sat together in the middle of the place. And when she'd finished off theirs, she'd come walking calmly through the awful stink of the plane's interior, the smell of sweat and puke and the spilt Elsan, and sit on my knee and wash herself clean, while the sun came up behind us, and the flat coast of Lincolnshire and the big tower of Wainfleet All Saints came pinkly out of the morning mist like the kingdom of Heaven.

She clung round Luke's neck all during debriefing, digging her claws into his old leather jacket. We were the last home, and the other crews usually hang around the debriefing hall, drinking their breakfast, which is supposed to be coffee but is usually stronger. Everybody gathered round open-mouthed; the little WAAF Intelligence officer just didn't know what to write down; she thought Luke was having her on about Dinah and the ME 110. So she summoned her Senior Man, and he summoned Groupie.

Groupie, or Group Captain Leonard Roy to you, ran our lot. Grey as a badger and too fat to get into a Wimpey, but no fool. He knew that cats shooting down ME 110s was against King's Regulations. But he also weighed up the sea of grinning faces. There hadn't been many grins round East Doddingham that winter. We'd lost a lot of planes, we were permanently frozen day and night, on the ground and in the air, the local pubs were hovels, and the most attractive local females were the horses. But above all, we were the forgotten men.

130

You see, Wimpeys, or Wellington bombers to you, were good old crates that took a lot of knocking out of the air. But they were old, and slow. Not as slow as Stirlings, thank God, that lumbered round the air like pregnant cows, and were Jerry's favourite food. Everybody cheered when they heard the Stirlings were going on an op, because it gave the rest of us a better chance of getting home. But a Wimpey only carries a tiny bomb load. One Lancaster carries as many bombs as five Wimpeys. Why put thirty Wimpey blokes up for the chop, when seven guys in a Lanc can do the same damage (or lack of it)?

But the great British public had to have its thousand-bomber raids on Happy Valley, so we were always sent in to make up the thousand . . .

Anyway, Groupie looks around all the happy faces and says, "Put the cat on the crew roster. Shilling a day for aircrew rations. These damn Wimpeys are always full of mice . . . "

It got a laugh; though everybody knew no mouse that valued its life would go near a Wimpey, corned beef crumbs or no corned beef crumbs.

She slept with Luke; she ate with Luke. Though in the mess hall, during an ops breakfast, she'd jump from table to table and get spoiled rotten with bacon rind and even whole bloody lumps of bacon. Because every other crew wanted her, especially after she helped Luke get his second Jerry. Aircrews were mascot-mad, you see. I mean, our last Wingco wouldn't *fly* without his old golf umbrella stuck behind his seat. He made a joke of it, of course, saying he could use it if his parachute failed to open. But the night his groundcrew mislaid it, just before a raid, he went as white as a sheet, and threw up right there on the tarmac. He still went on the raid; but he didn't come back. I saw him buy it with a direct flak hit, over the marshalling yards at Hamm. None of his crew got out.

We all had something. Hoppy had a rabbit's foot. Mike had a very battered golliwog. Bog had a penknife, with all the paint worn off, where he turned it over and over in his pocket during a raid.

But all the attempts to get Dinah away from Luke failed. Even the kidnap attempt by G-George. Dinah had been missing all day, before that night. We'd had to practically carry Luke out to the plane, because he was quite certain that without her, we were for the chop. Then, as were waiting our turn in the queue for take-off, we saw G-George taxiing past, trying to jump the queue. That was their undoing. We saw it all quite clearly, because it was bright moonlight. Wimpeys have these little triangular windows all along their sides. Dinah's little white face appeared at one of them. And those windows are just celluloid. We saw her white paws scrabbling, then the window was out, and she leapt down and ran to us like a Derby winner. Luke, warned over the intercom, swung his turret hard left, exposing the armoured doors behind him. He opened the doors and she jumped in, and he closed the doors and swung the turret back, and we were off to Essen.

She got her third Jerry that night. After that, the Ministry of Information let in the reporters and photographers, and the legend of East Doddingham Dinah was born, with photographs of her clinging to Luke for grim life, and daft headlines like: DODDINGHAM DINAH HUNTS THE HUN.

You'd think, the way they went on, that she and Luke had shot down half the Jerry air force. But they only got four; all told. Still, I suppose it was good for the Home Front and the War Effort. Until some nut began to write to the papers, suggesting that all rear gunners carried a cat. The Air Ministry stamped on the whole stunt after that.

But she did much more marvellous things than just helping Luke shoot down night fighters. She *knew* things. Like the night she walked aboard, and then walked off again. I was just revving up, when she went to the exit hatch and began to claw at it, and give little silent miaows through the roar of the engines, *pleading* to be out.

God, the crew went *crazy* over the intercom. Should we let her out or shouldn't we? The row got so bad they even noticed in the control tower.

We all knew what it meant. She was our luck. If she went, we were for the chop, full stop . . .

Oddly enough, it was Luke who settled it. I heard his shaking voice through my headphones, he was very Yorkshire in his agony.

"She volunteered for aircrew duties, and she can bloody volunteer out an' all. Aah'm not tekkin' her against her will."

And nobody stopped him, when he undid the door clips and she dropped to the ground and shot off towards the warmth of the groundcrew hut.

We took off in a silence like a funeral; we went up to seven thousand in a silence like a funeral. Then Mike, the flight engineer, glancing over my shoulder at the dials said, quietly, "Port engine's acting up, skipper!"

Well, it was. A fraction. Temperature a degree or so too hot; losing a few revs, then gaining a few, without either of us touching the throttles. But B-Baker was old, like I said. And it was the kind of acting-up that usually stopped, if you flew on for a bit. We'd been to Berlin and back on worse. And it was certainly the kind of fault which would vanish the moment you turned back to the airfield. Leaving you with egg all over your face, and a very nasty interview with Groupie. That was always the way when a guy's nerve began to go... the slippery slope which ended with you lying on your bunk, gibbering like a baby under the bedclothes till they came to take you away and reduce you to the rank of AC2 and put you on cleaning the airfield bogs. Lack of Moral Fibre, they said at your court martial – LMF for short.

"*Leave* it," I snarled at Mike.

We flew on; crossed the English coast. I could feel Mike watching that dial, over my shoulder. The rest of them were still like a funeral over the intercom.

Then Luke said, "She always was keen to come before, skipper . . . "

And Hoppy said, "We've done forty-two missions without a gripe. They owe us one . . . "

I turned back. Immediately, the bloody port engine settled down; and ran as sweet as a sewing machine, all the way home.

I was in Groupie's office next morning, having a strip torn off me, when we heard the bang, right through the brick walls. We ran out together. But across the airfield, on her dispersal pad, poor B-Baker was already a write-off.

The sergeant of my groundcrew had been revving up the port engine of his darling to demonstrate her innocence. When a prop blade snapped off clean at the shaft. Went through the cockpit, shaving a slice off his backside, and straight out the other side into the main petrol tank in the starboard wing. Which promptly caught fire. He got away with a well-singed skin, and one and a half buttocks. He was lucky; he was on the ground at the time. In the air, we wouldn't have had a prayer . . .

We never worked out how Dinah *knew*. There were those clever-cuts who reckoned she'd felt the different vibes from the duff propeller through the pads of her paws, the moment she got on board.

We reckoned she just *knew*.

Like she knew about O-Oboe.

I mean, she was always prowling around the aircraft on their dispersal pads. As I said before, she could jump as if she could almost fly. A two-metre jump to a wing root was nothing to her. She would chat up the groundcrews as they serviced the engines, and never say no to grub (though she got no fatter). Then she would go for a trot along the top of the fuselage, or wash

133

herself in the occasional bleak glimpse of February sun, on top of a cockpit canopy. I mean, any crate, not just our brand-new B-Baker. The other crews in the squadron liked that; they reckoned she was spreading her luck round a bit. And certainly, in her first two months with the squadron, we lost no planes at all. (Though of course the snow and fog cut our bombing missions down a lot in those two months.)

But it was different with O-Oboe. Next to us, Dinah was fonder of Pip Percival's crew than any other. She was always running round O-Oboe. It was parked next to us at dispersals.

It happened after breakfast one morning. O-Oboe's groundcrew sergeant came into my little squadron office, looking . . . upset.

"I think Dinah's ill, sir. She's sitting up on O-Oboe, an' she won't come down, even for bacon."

I got Luke, and we went across in my jeep. When we were still quite a way from O-Oboe, Luke whistled and said, "Christ, look at that!"

He meant O-Oboe. Through the mist, she looked like a ghost. She looked . . . cold. She looked as if her wheels weren't really touching the ground. She looked like you could walk straight through her.

You probably think I'm talking nonsense. Surely on a misty morning, *all* the planes would look like that? But our new B-Baker next to O-Oboe looked just misty and oily and *solid*. We both knew what that ghostly look meant. O-Oboe was for the chop, on her next mission. We all got very twitchy about things like that. There were bunks where every guy who dared sleep in them got the chop straight away. There were Nissen huts where whole crews who dared live in them got the chop straight away. After a while, nobody would sleep in those particular bunks. After a while, a wise wing commander would turn that Nissen hut over to storing NAAFI supplies. There was even a beautiful WAAF on the station, all of whose boyfriends got the chop. Nobody would go near her. In the end, in despair, she got herself pregnant by a local farmer; as he married her, it was a happier ending than most . . .

Anyway, we knew O-Oboe was for it. And on top of O-Oboe, on the cockpit canopy, Dinah was sitting. Not washing herself as usual, but sitting hunched-up, eyes shut, ears down, forehead wrinkled. We called up to her; she never stirred. She must have been there for hours; there were beads of mist on the tips of her fur.

Luke climbed slitheringly up and got her. He wouldn't have done it for anything but Dinah. Nobody even wants to *touch* an aircraft that's due for the chop . . .

She was shivering. We took her into the squadron office and warmed her at the stove, and checked that all her legs worked and she wasn't hurt. We warmed up the milk ration, and she drank that. Her nose was cold and wet. She seemed quite normal. So we let her out . . .

She went straight back to O-Oboe, sitting in the same place.

Luke fetched her back four more times. And each time she went back. In the end, Luke said, "She's not ill. She's just *grieving*. For O-Oboe."

After that, we kept her shut up in a cupboard, with a blanket, till take-off. But it was too late. Word had got around. Nobody looked at O-Oboe's crew during the briefing. A sort of space opened up around them at ops breakfast (which, confusingly, we eat at night, just before take-off). You could tell they knew they'd had it.

They didn't come back. Crews who know they're for the chop never come back.

After that, the groundcrews took against Dinah. When she appeared round their aircraft when they were servicing it, they shooed her away. She didn't understand, and kept coming back. They began throwing things at her.

From being the queen of the wing, she'd become the angel of death. The first we knew of it was when she came into my office limping, with one ear torn, and her back soaked with dirty engine oil. Luke spent a whole day cleaning her up. But we didn't dare let her out of my office any more; till it was time to go on a mission.

And the new Wingco told me she'd have to go. Our losses were starting to climb again, because the weather was better, and we were flying more missions. But the wing as a whole blamed Dinah; Dinah had turned against them, and was bringing bad luck. Some bastard tried running her down with a jeep in the dark, as she was actually following us across the runway to B-Baker . . .

Luke took her to live with his aunty in Doncaster; I drove them across in the jeep. We sneaked out and left her lying asleep by a roaring fire, with a saucer of milk by her nose. We were sad, but she'd be safe there, and she'd done her bit for the War Effort.

Half an hour after we left, she vanished through aunty's open bathroom window. Two nights later, she turned up at dispersal, in time for the flight. Forty miles of strange countryside she'd crossed, in two days. And spot on time for the op.

It was to be her last op. The funny thing was, she walked aboard as calm as ever . . .

A new target. The U-boat pens at L'Orient, on the French coast. Should have been an easy one – over the sea all the way, after going as far as Land's End to confuse the German radar. Then into the top end of the Bay of Biscay, and on to L'Orient at zero height from the sea.

Jerry had Junkers 88s out over the bay, waiting for us. Ours came in from above, for a change. If Dinah hadn't made the most incredible leap off Luke's knee to touch the top of his turret, he'd never have seen the one that nearly got us. But Luke didn't waste his chance. The bastard made off for home with one engine stopped, and glycol steaming from the other; I doubt he made it.

He was Dinah's fourth and last. The flak was hell over L'Orient; they were waiting for us. Thirty seconds before bombs-gone we took a 35mm cannonshell amidships. Bob was badly hurt; and Hoppy a bit, and Hoppy's radio set burst into flames. I never knew where our bombs went; probably into the local fish and chip shop. It was just good, with a fire aboard, to know they were gone. We went skidding on over France, with me shouting, "Bail out, bail out!" and trying to make enough height so that the parachutes would open, before the plane blew up or broke in half.

Because, above all, aircrew are terrified of fire. I mean, it's one thing to die; it's another thing to burn slowly . .

So it's all the more credit to Hoppy and Bob that they stayed and fought the blaze, fanned by a gale blowing in through the shell holes. Hoppy tried to rip the wireless set loose and throw it through the window, with his mittened hands. That's why he hasn't got much in the way of hands any more. In the end, the set burned its way through its mountings and out through the side of the crate, and all we were left with was a hurricane blowing through the fuselage, and two badly injured blokes . . . I went down to zero feet again and got out over the Bay as quickly as possible.

I was so busy trying to keep the crate in the air, and Mike was so busy getting morphine into Bob and Hoppy that we were nearly back over England before we realised that Luke hadn't said a word. I sent Mike back to look . . .

The rear turret was turned hard left. The armoured doors were open. Of Luke and Dinah there was no sign . . .

Luke had bailed out when I told him to. He was even more frightened of fire than the rest of us.

I got B-Baker down on a Coastal Command field near Land's End; but the fire had weakened the fuselage, and she broke in half on impact. Goodbye, B-Baker. Goodbye, Bob and Hoppy, for a long stay in hospital (though Bob made a good recovery eventually). Goodbye to my bomb aimer and front gunner, a kid called Harris who doesn't really come into this story. He'd bailed out through the front hatch when I told him, and finished the war in Stalag Luft XII. And goodbye, Luke and Dinah. Or so I thought.

Wingco put Bob and Hoppy in for the Air Force Cross, and sent me and Mike home for a month's leave to get over it. It was the end of April, and the nights were getting too short for raids into Germany. The crates were being changed from black night-camouflage to brown-and-green day-camouflage, and the crews were getting new training, for day-bombing and no one seemed to want two bomb-happy odds-and-sods. It's not usual for the Air Ministry to be so generous, but we'd nearly finished two tours of duty. Anyway, I had a nice time at home, doing up my parents' garden, which had gone to pot with the old man being on war work. And watching a bit of scratch county cricket, while the world got ready for D-Day without me.

I was weeding away in the back garden, hands all soil, when my mother said there was someone to see me.

It was Luke, shy and grinning as ever. Just looking a bit thin, that's all.

"Dinah?" I asked, dread in my heart, after I'd finished banging him on the back.

He grinned again. "She's still catching up," he said. And he told me all about it.

He'd got down safely in the chute, with Dinah clutched tight in his arms, though he almost lost her with the jerk when the chute opened. But she'd shot off immediately, when she sensed people coming, on the ground.

Fortunately, they'd been decent French people, and they'd passed him on to the underground network that got British fliers safely out of the country.

He'd admitted he hadn't enjoyed the network much. Flying crates was one thing. Walking and cycling through Occupied France, with a beret on his head, and civvy clothes was another. He'd kept his air-force tunic on, under his overcoat, but he was still scared the Jerries would shoot him as a spy if they caught him. And the endless waiting in the dark in barns and cellars . . .

It was Dinah who'd kept him going. She'd followed him all the way across France. When things got roughest, when he'd had to follow his guide past German patrols, she'd suddenly appear, poking her white head over a wall, or trotting along the road in front. Sometimes, when he had a long wait in some cellar or barn, she'd slip in to visit him. He was scared for her, too. Because the French were pretty hungry by that time, and were eating cats as a treat at Christmas. He said there wasn't another cat to be seen anywhere, and when people were offered rabbit pie in restaurants they made silent "miaow" noises with their mouths.

But she'd stayed with him, as far as the Spanish frontier. And then the really incredible thing had happened.

The night they'd crossed into Spain, in the foothills of the Pyrenees, they'd been driven to earth by a last border patrol of German soldiers accompanied by the local Vichy policemen. Luke had lain with his cheek pressed into the earth, while the patrol passed. But the last Jerry had lingered, been suspicious of the clump of bushes Luke was lying in. Had seemed to sense, beyond all sense, that there was something alive in there. And then Luke, unable to hold his

138

breath any longer, had taken a deep one, and made a dead twig lying underneath him snap. The Jerry had taken two paces towards the bushes, raised his rifle, called to the others . . .

When out had stepped Dinah, with even a damned mouse in her mouth.

Luke said the Jerry must've been a cat lover. He made a great fuss of Dinah, stroked her, called her "liebling". The other Jerries had laughed at him, then called him after them, saying they hadn't got all night.

And so Luke had passed into Spain, and then the greater safety of Portugal. And still Dinah had been with him, at a distance.

He'd told the whole story to the British Consul in Lisbon, sure of getting Dinah a lift in the stripped-down bomber that flew the guys home.

The consul had been very snotty, and talked about rabies regulations, and refused.

Luke needn't have worried. They were halfway up Biscay before she emerged from the piled-up blankets of the crew's rest bed. And the crew, being good blokes, agreed to let her slip off at Hendon.

I looked at my watch. My parents lived "somewhere in the home counties" as we used to say for security purposes in those days. And Hendon was only thirty miles away.

"She'll find me," said Luke. "You'll see!"

"Better stay here with us till she does. We don't want her having to walk all the way to East Doddingham. She'll be tired."

I don't think either of us had the slightest doubt . . .

Early the second morning, she dropped on to Luke's bed through the open dormer window.

She should have come back to East Doddingham in triumph. You'd have thought they'd have put her story in the papers. But our old Groupie had gone where good groupies go, planning new forward air bases in the France that was soon to be liberated. There was a new Groupie that knew not Dinah. And the smell of Victory was in the air already, and with it that smell of peacetime bullshit that was the scourge of the RAF.

On the air station where she'd been queen, where they'd begged for a tuft of her fur for luck, or a carefully-hoarded dropped whisker, Dinah had become no more than a rabies risk. We offered to have a whip-round in the Wing, to pay for her stay in quarantine. But such nonsense was not to be tolerated; there was a war to win. Dinah must be destroyed.

There wasn't time for anything subtle. We met the RAF policeman, as he carried Dinah out in a dirty great cage form the guardroom. It was quite simple. I knocked him cold, and Luke took the cage and ran.

They didn't court martial me, for striking an other-rank. Perhaps they were scared the story of Dinah would come out. They diagnosed me as suffering from combat fatigue, and I flew a desk for the rest of the war.

We had our first crew reunion in 1948. It took Hoppy that long to arrange it, when they finally stopped operating on what was left of his hands. Everybody but Luke was there. The Air Ministry was not helpful about Luke. They had finally caught up with him in 1945, when he returned home for his mother's funeral. He'd spent some time in the glasshouse, then got a dishonourable discharge.

We found him in 1950. He'd managed to get to Northern Ireland with Dinah; she'd stowed away on the Belfast-Laugharne ferry, following him as he knew she would. They walked together in the freedom of the Irish Republic. He'd found work as a farm hand, till his mother died.

He'd not seen Dinah since; though there'd been talk of a white cat that hung around the glasshouse gate. But when he finally got out, she'd gone. Tired of waiting perhaps. Or knocked down by a lorry.

The following year we decided at the reunion to drive down to East Doddingham. We wished we hadn't. God, what a mess. The guardroom was roofless. The runways were crumbling, and being used by men on Sunday afternoons to teach their wives to drive. The field itself was back under turnips, and the hangars were being used as grain stores. The RAF had found East Doddingham expendable, as it had always found us.

But Luke swore he'd seen a glimpse of Dinah. A white head peeping above the parapet of what had once been B-Baker's dispersal. Nobody else saw her; but we pretended to believe him.

Funny thing is, we've gone down to East Doddingham for our reunion ever since. God knows why. It's a dump. The accommodation in the pub is awful, and the beer still tastes like piss, as it always did.

But every year, somebody reckons that they see Dinah. We never see her when we're all together. But there's always someone who goes for a last solitary sentimental stroll round the old field. And then they come back and say they've seen her. But she always vanishes immediately. She never comes across to say hello.

I saw a white cat myself, this year. Staring at me over the broken concrete with huge dark unfathomable eyes, set in a head like a beautiful skull. It *can't* be her; she'd be over forty years old, and no cat lives that long.

But maybe she went back to the field in 1945, when it was already running down, and nobody remained who remembered her (life was perilously short in the RAF). Maybe she lived in peace at last, and raised kittens. Maybe this was her daughter, or granddaughter.

Or maybe she was a ghost. Or maybe she just lives on in the fond memory and failing eyesight of ageing aircrew.

But she certainly wasn't a ghost in 1944.

HIGHLY-TRAINED "PLATOON" OF GUIDE CATS IN VIETNAM

ANONYMOUS

A SQUAD, upon being ordered to move out, was led off in all different directions by the cats; on many occasions the animals led their troops racing through thick bush in pursuit of field mice . . . often the animals would stalk and attack . . . the dangling packstraps of the soldier immediately in front of them. If the weather was inclement, or even threatening inclemency, the cats were never anywhere to be found.

THE CAT AND ENDINGS

INDEPENDENCE BROWN

STELLA WHITELAW

INDEPENDENCE BROWN was her name right from the very beginning. The name sounded like the heroine of an early American pioneer film and it suited her. They could almost imagine her trekking across the plains of Arizona in a covered wagon, repelling Indians and enduring great hardships.

The Browns called her Independence in the first place because they got her on July 4 and were sorry about the American Revolution and the Boston Tea Party. But it soon became obvious that the tiny scruff of mottled fur was a fiercely independent and ornery cuss from the word go, determined to stand forever on her own wobbly four paws.

She did everything in her own time. Lifted onto a lap, the kitten fought furiously for release, only to return minutes later, acquiescent and docile. Put on a litter tray, she scrambled out, granules flying over the floor, only to sit politely by the door asking to be let out. Food and drink were ignored: she ate when she wanted to, be it dawn or midnight.

It took the family a long time to get to know her; if they met outside, Inde merely glanced at them as if they were strangers.

"I sometimes wonder if that cat belongs to us at all," said Mrs Ellen Brown. "She gives us all the cold shoulder."

142

Inde grew into a striking British silver tabby. The dark symmetrical markings on her grey fur were like blotting-paper images, and the lines and splodges on her small face gave her a curiously clown like look. It was perhaps this frivolous appearance that she was determined to live down.

The only person Inde acknowledged was Corrine Brown — if acknowledge was the right word. They had something strongly in common and recognized in each other a kindred spirit. At sixteen, Corrine was going through a fight for her independence, and she often envied Inde's ruthless demolition of any Brown plans for her life.

Several times they made an appointment for a very necessary visit to the vet's. Inde refused point-blank to go. She was up and over the garden wall and into the woods, and was not seen again for thirty-six hours. Then one day she climbed into her travelling basket and sat there waiting for Mr Brown to get the car out. When she was brought home, she sat groggily licking the sore place with an air of comical sadness, as if she knew all about denied kittens and the lost joys of motherhood.

That evening she curled up on Corrine's lap all through a James Bond film. They thought that at last Inde had mellowed. But they were wrong. The next day she had recovered, and spat at anything that moved.

The neighbouring woods were her delight. She played and explored and scavenged. Every square inch was known territory. As the woods changed with the seasons, so Inde found further joys and excitements. She flew down the garden with the long rippling strides of a tiger, took the wall with the graceful leap of a front runner at the Grand National, sped across the stepping-stones of the brook with the sure-footedness of a gazelle. Corrine never failed to feel a surge of admiration watching this co-ordination of movement; it was beautiful. She would look up from her studies and watch from the window as Inde took her path to freedom. Corrine sometimes fancied she could share the joy of the cat as Inde headed for the woods. Corrine wished she knew where she herself was going, and what lay beyond school examinations and perhaps university.

Inde deliberately strengthened her independence. During her periodic disappearances, they did not look for her. Her return to bed and board was heralded by a sharp *yeowell* at the back door. She did not apologize for the wisps of dry fern and moss clinging to her fur; she had been roaming her beloved woods.

"I can't think what's got into Inde these days," said Ellen Brown with some exasperation as she threw away an untouched dish of cat-food. "She's always

143

had eccentric eating habits, but she's never ignored food altogether."

Corrine went on her knees to stroke the cat. There was something odd about Inde. She was creeping around as if half-expecting to be set upon, front paws held out in a curiously stiff manner. Inde licked the salt off Corrine's fingers with her rough sandpaper tongue. It was the first sign of affection she had ever shown.

Corrine put some morsels of chicken in the palm of her hand and held them under Inde's nose. The small tongue shot out and the chicken was gone in a flash. The cat was starving.

"Well, I never," said Ellen from the pastry board. "She ignored it all yesterday."

Corrine filled a dish and put it at Inde's toes. The cat crouched down on her haunches and polished off the lot. It was the same with some milk.

"How strange," said Corrine, worried. It was so unlike Inde, to have to be waited on. Her spirit was fiercely valiant, but something was defeating her now. "Perhaps we ought to take her to the vet."

"Give it a day or two and see if she gets over it," said Ellen. "I've a heavy week. Two committee meetings and a flag day."

And Corrine was busy packing. She had collected the right number of grades and was to read history for three years. Her parents had hoped she would accept a place in London so that she could still live at home, but Corrine had opted for a university in the industrial north. She was apprehensive about the move. What would she find there? What would the people be like? She knew she must take her courage into her two hands and run at it, in the same way that Inde ran to her beloved woods.

Corrine took Inde upstairs with her. She felt in the need of uncritical company. She was on the defensive, with her mother still trying to organize everything for her. She started to sort out her books so that she knew which ones to leave at home, making a list of their titles.

It was an absorbing task and the two piles of books grew, hiding Inde from view. Suddenly the piles fell over and Inde shot across the room; she crashed headlong into a record case, fur flying and paws askew. Inde stepped back and crouched on the carpet, trembling, her long ringed tail swished from side to side. But it was not in anger. It was more like the sweeping of a radar beam.

Corrine walked on her knees to the stricken cat and tried to calm her.

"Easy, girl," she soothed. "Did the silly old books frighten you? There . . . there . . . "

She looked carefully at the cat from all angles, ran her hands down each limb, then she put a cushion on the floor and moved away to the other side of the room. A kind of chill settled on her actions. She tapped the leg of her bed with a pencil and called out: "Inde . . . Inde . . . "

Inde got up, ears perked forward, whiskers twitching. She did not leap over the cushion or step across it. She did not side-track either. She walked straight into it.

Corrine picked up Inde gently and sat on the floor, cradling her in her arms. Silently tears fell down her cheeks. She had never felt so sad in all her life. A light had gone out, Inde's light. The light of Independence Brown. The cat was blind.

The vet thought Inde must have been in an accident during one of her disappearances. Perhaps a car wing had caught her a sharp blow to the side of the head; perhaps she had fallen from a high tree and detached the retina. They would never know. The vet suggested that the kindest thing would be to have her put down.

Inde was carefully exploring the vet's examination table, sniffing the edges, alert and curious. The afternoon sunlight streamed through the windows, catching all the silver in her coat. Her fur was alive and sparkling. No one could destroy anything so beautiful.

"Oh no, I think we'll give her a chance," said Ellen Brown slowly. "She's got such an independent nature."

At first they moved every awkward object in the house out of the way — the umbrella stand, the log basket, waste bins. Then they realized that this was not really doing the cat a favour. It was better that Inde learned where everything was and tracked round them. Everyone became consciously tidier, no longer leaving shopping, briefcases, shoes on the floor.

Inde responded to noise; she recognized the sound of the tin-opener, the refrigerator door being opened, milk poured. She kept out of the way when the telephone rang or there was a knock on the door. She became far more vocal. If she was quite lost, she stood still in that foreign place, miaowing for someone to put her somewhere more familiar.

By the time Corrine came home from her first term at university, Inde had come to terms with her blindness. She still walked with a strange gait as if she was not completely relaxed, but her independence had reasserted itself and she did not want to be helped. She knew the lay-out of the house and garden intimately, only thrown occasionally by someone's carelessness. She still ruled her own life. She had no intention of being an invalid.

One day Corrine found Inde sitting by the foot of the garden wall. She looked melancholy, as far as a clown-faced cat can look melancholy. She let out a single, sad wail.

"Why, I believe you are missing your woods," said Corrine. "You know they are over there, don't you, the other side of the wall? Poor Inde, you can smell them and hear them but you can't cope with that wall. You need a helping hand."

She lifted Inde up to put her over the wall, but the cat struggled and flopped out of her grasp, falling onto the waste ground the other side. Inde streaked off into the undergrowth, careering headlong through grass and fern like a demented creature. Even when she was out of sight Corrine could still hear the small sounds of her crashing progress through the woods.

Corrine hung about, but Inde did not come back. Eventually she gave up and went indoors. Late that evening they heard a piercing *yeowell*. It was Inde waiting to be returned over the wall. She was wet. She had obviously tried to cross the stepping-stones and fallen in the brook.

"Well, I'm much too busy to ferry her backwards and forwards over the wall," said Ellen. "I can't be around to do wall duty every day. What's going to happen when you go back to university?"

"I'll think of something."

It did not seem feasible to knock a hole in the wall, so Corrine devised two planks leaning against the wall, one either side, so that Inde could get back. She wedged the foot of each plank with a stone and introduced Inde to her walk-over. Inde sniffed, then after a few hesitant, tentative steps, she understood. When she got to the top of the wall, she sniffed the air, not sure

146

what was expected of her. She was about to leap off when Corrine restrained her.

"Oh, no, you don't. You've got to learn the way down too. Then you'll be able to get back." Corrine guided the cat to the edge of the plank that led down to the ground. Inde stepped forward with perfect trust. She caught on immediately and sped down the plank. Without a murmur of thanks she darted off into the woods with rather more care for the undergrowth.

Corrine stood there, laughing. She had given Inde a bridge to freedom. She wondered if someone would give her a bridge into this new adult world she had so recently entered.

Inde never hesitated again. She flew down the garden, unerringly straight for the plank, up and over and into the woods. No one would have known that she was blind. It was a joy to watch the animal flying through the air.

One night there was a gale and the wind and heavy rain dislodged the planks. Inde shot out of the back door, straight down the garden but pulled up short of the wall. She sniffed around and found the fallen plank and sat on it, waiting for someone to do something about it.

A young Canadian student, Bruce, was staying overnight. After breakfast he went down the garden with Corrine to look at the damage.

"Well, if I'm going to be an architect, I might as well start my career with a cat bridge," he grinned. He put stakes in the ground at intervals and lashed the planks to the stakes. It was firm but amateurish.

"If I had more time I'd build a brick-supported ramp," he said, wielding a mallet on the stakes. Inde sat at a safe distance, listening to the noise with concealed curiosity. "Though it seems a lot of work just to get one cat over one wall."

"It's all in the name of independence," said Corrine, mysteriously. "You could always come again in the spring holiday," she added.

"So I could," he said.

The bridge was Inde's lifeline to freedom. Over the years Bruce made adaptations and improvements to its design. Inde took to each change with trust and confidence. She now knew every inch of the woods. It was still difficult to believe that she could not see. She did not let her blindness stop her doing anything she wanted to do. She even climbed trees, moving carefully along swaying branches. Sometimes Corrine watched with her heart in her mouth as Inde took a calculated leap into the air to reach another branch. Sometimes the cat missed.

She learned the size and position of each of the stepping-stones and could

147

walk across them with scarcely a hesitation. Her mind was a complicated file of maps and routes and angles, all painstakingly learned by trial and error, committed to memory, and once there, acted upon with total confidence.

In her first year of teaching Corrine came home regularly, but gradually there were other countries with sites of historical interest to see, new friends to visit, holidays with Bruce. Inde accepted that her dearest friend should be finding new worlds and had less time for her. She turned to Ellen and grew closer to her.

Ellen was slowing down her good work for the community as younger and more enthusiastic women moved into the neighbourhood. She sat more often in the garden with her sewing or writing letters, Inde stretched out on the grass beside her, the sun warming her body.

"I'm quite glad I've given up all those committees," said Ellen. "I can enjoy my own garden now without having to get up and rush off somewhere."

Absent-mindedly she put her hand down to stroke the cat's head. Inde put out her tongue and licked at Ellen's fingers. It was the first time that Inde had ever shown any sign of affection towards Ellen and she was unaccountably touched. All those years of tapping saucers and leading the cat with her voice; all those years of watching and caring for the independent creature had not gone completely unnoticed.

She stroked the cat's chin. There was the faintest vibration in Inde's throat. It was the birth of a purr. Ellen felt rewarded beyond measure.

"Both of us getting old," she teased. "Soft thing   "

Inde had an annual check-up at the vet's. He thought she was remarkably fit despite her disability and her age. "A touch of arthritis," he said. "But that's to be expected at her age. Keep an eye on her if we have a very cold snap this winter."

Corrine came home for the whole of the summer vacation. She was packing again. This time she was off to Australia on a teacher-exchange scheme. It was an exciting prospect. They were even going to exchange flats, and Corrine would be living in Sydney not far from the sea.

As Corrine's world grew, so Inde's shrank. She did not wander so far now. She had got thinner and the bright silver in her coat had dulled. She stood on the doorstep facing the garden, her face lifted towards the sun and towards the life that used to exist beyond.

"I think she wants to go to the woods," said Corrine. "Shall I take her? She used to love them so." Corrine began to stroll down the garden. "Inde . . . Come on, Inde . . . "

Inde followed stiffly. The bottom of the garden seemed a long way. Corrine bent to carry her over the wall, but the cat struggled out of her arms and insisted on crossing the bridge by herself, slowly and a little unsteadily.

"All right, have it your own way," said Corrine.

They wandered through the woods together, the cat sniffing old haunts and new growth, remembering all the joys that had once been hers; oak moss, leaf mould, wild violets; Corrine thinking of the new paths that were opening up for her, if she had the courage to take them.

When they came to the brook, Inde hesitated. She had forgotten the exact sequence of the stepping-stones. Corrine went ahead, tapping each stone and calling. Inde followed. Once she almost slipped, but Corrine was there to catch her and set her back on the stone. Inde took a great leap from the last stone onto the opposite bank. That much she remembered.

It was a lovely afternoon for both of them, golden and warm; the silver cat's splodges and stripes merging with the dappled shadows until she was almost part of the woods themselves.

Inde was very tired by the time they got home. She drank some milk and stretched herself out before the newly lit fire and went to sleep, her paws still twitching with memories of her old exciting life.

"I suppose I may not see Inde again," said Corrine, her hand faltering on the soft fur, feeling the gentle rise and fall of that stubborn heart. How quickly the years had gone by, and Corrine had become too busy sometimes to give any time to her cat. Every day Inde had lived in her shadowy world, day after day, refusing to give in, following the promise in the wind.

"Probably not," said Ellen, turning her face away.

Corrine continued to stroke the silver coat, remembering the cat's endless courage and determination; her fight for everything that she had a right to have. "You'll stay with her, won't you?" She said in a low voice.

"I'll be here," said Ellen.

The following week Corrine left for Australia. She did not hesitate. Her plane flew unerringly straight, up and over, taking her across a bridge to freedom.

From THE DEATH OF GRANDMA

JUDY GARDINER

A SHORT while ago, I said that I didn't believe that cat families had leaders, but I do remember one cat that had an awful lot of *influence*. It was a rather battered old soul with only one eye, who was called Grandma. (Presumably she had started off with another name, but after years of steadily producing kittens no one could remember it.) Still, Grandma was given the respect to which her age and fecundity entitled her, being the only cat out of the resident eight that was allowed to sit on the kitchen dresser.

I spent a lot of time one summer watching Grandma with the other cats, and on first acquaintance she seemed a rather overpowering, interfering sort. Two of the other cats had kittens, and although they appeared perfectly competent to deal with them, the old girl insisted on doing all the washing and, later on, the toilet-training. Once or twice I thought I saw the mothers flush with annoyance but they didn't argue, which at the time I regarded as a bit feeble of them.

151

It took several weeks to recognise the heart of gold beneath the bossy exterior and to realise that it wasn't always a case of Grandma sticking her oar in. She was a skilful hunter for instance, always bringing in rabbits and pheasants from the fields and setting them down in the barn for the other cats to share, and she was the only one of the eight who learned to manipulate the old finger-latches on the farmhouse doors. Kittens used to ask her to let them in (or out) and if there were no human beings within easy distance she would generally comply.

Because everyone had great faith in Grandma's high level of common sense no one worried unduly when she didn't turn up for supper one night. The other cats appeared equally undismayed. During the course of the next day we called her and searched round the farmyard, some of the other cats came too, but only in a benevolent, rather jokey sort of way. By supper-time that night the empty space on the corner of the dresser was beginning to get on everyone's nerves.

We'd been asleep for hours when the noise woke us; a weird hollow keening like a ghost wind sobbing at the gates of hell. It wailed on and on, this blending of unearthly voices that seemed to be coming from somewhere out in the fields. We pulled on trousers and jerseys and followed the sound, very apprehensive of what we might find.

We found the cats, all of them huddled in a tight pack round Grandma. They still kept on with their awful broken wailing and it can only have been my horrified imagination that made it sound as if they were forming consonants and fluttering little fragments of words. In the light of the torches we saw that Grandma was in a gin-trap, that she had a broken back and that she was still alive.

And this is the part that will haunt me for ever: they wouldn't let us touch her. One of the friends who was with us had had veterinary experience, and although he tried with all the skill and gentleness at his command to release her, the cats wouldn't let him, even though they knew him and normally trusted him. It just seemed as if they hated us quite savagely for intruding on their private grief.

So we had to leave. And when we went back at first light Grandma was dead and the other cats had gone.

MOURNING ONE (MING'S DEATH)

BRUCE FOGLE

FOR THE first three days (after Ming's death) Chan and Mitsou looked everywhere for him, and expected us every time that we came back to the flat, to bring him back. After three days the pattern changed. Ming always sat or lay in a particular place on the left of the fireplace. Now neither of the other two cats will sit there, or even walk across it. They laid out Ming's favourite toys there – two pink catnip mice – and they sit for hours on the other side of the fireplace apparently "talking" to something that we cannot see. They have both completely calmed down, but they are upset if anybody moves Ming's mice. To see what would happen, we have deliberately moved these and put them elsewhere in the room at night before going to bed – but the next morning they are back in their proper place, and they are there now as I write. Nor do the cats like anybody standing there, and on occasions I have done so to light the fire and, looking up, have seen expressions of horror on the cats' faces, as if I was treading on Ming. The same thing has happened to my wife and to the girl who comes in twice a week to help keep the place clean.

I have the very distinct impression that dear old Ming is still about.

MOURNING TWO (KYM)

JOYCE STRANGER

THE HOUSE was dead.
 No purring cat to greet us. No raucous shout of anger or dismay or amusement as he appeared. We burned all his possessions, Viking-like, unable to face them.

We went indoors, but there was nothing for us there. Only Anne and I were at home. We went out, had a meal out, went shopping and came in to get a meal no one wanted at all.

That night I dreamed I was in a wood and Kym was running away from me. His cries grew fainter and fainter as I ran calling, calling, calling. Then they stopped and I woke, knowing this time the dream was true and no amount of calling would bring him back.

I went down into the silent kitchen.

It was time for Anne to go back to college. After she had gone, and the men had gone to work, the house was very still. Uncannily still. I looked into the garden and there under the veronica bush, I saw Kym. I stared. He didn't move.

Unbelieving, I went into the garden. There couldn't be a cat there. But there was.

Next door's black cat stared up at me, safely ensconced in Kym's favourite place. I looked at the heather bed and there was a tabby cat I had never seen before in my life. A ginger cat crouched on the fence. Another black cat was under the winter jasmine.

There were cats everywhere I looked. Eight of them, watching me, in an uncanny silence. Four I knew. They had all been Kym's enemies, warned off his territory. Now they were staking claims. Or were they mourning?

I didn't know. I remembered how Kym had gone across the road when Sandy died.

I knew I couldn't stand the silent house and haunted garden and I went out, to nowhere, to wander round the shops, not wanting to come home to a house where nothing moved except myself.

He had been dead for only two days and both were pointless and endless. I didn't care if all the carpets were ripped and all the paper torn off the walls. Just so long as there was a small live thing to rush and greet me when I came home, and to teach as I taught Kym, to come around with us.

"Where can I get another Siamese cat?" I asked the vet.

LAST WORDS TO A DUMB FRIEND

THOMAS HARDY

Pet was never mourned as you,
Purrer of the spotless hue,
Plumy tail, and wistful gaze
While you humoured our queer ways,
Or outshrilled your morning call
Up the stairs and through the hall –
Foot suspended in its fall –
While, expectant, you would stand
Arched, to meet the stroking hand;
Till your way you chose to wend
Yonder, to your tragic end.

Never another pet for me!
Let your place all vacant be;
Better blankness day by day
Than companion torn away.
Better bid his memory fade,
Better blot each mark he made,
Selfishly escape distress
By contrived forgetfulness,
Than preserve his prints to make
Every morn and eve an ache.

From the chair whereon he sat
Sweep his fur, nor wince thereat;
Rake his little pathways out
Mid the bushes roundabout;
Smooth away his talons' mark
From the claw-worn pine-tree bark,
Where he climbed as dusk embrowned,
Waiting us who loitered round.

Strange it is this speechless thing,
Subject to our mastering,
Subject for his life and food
To our gift, and time, and mood;
Timid pensioner of us Powers,
His existence ruled by ours,
Should – by crossing at a breath
Into safe and shielded death,
By the merely taking hence
Of his insignificance –
Loom as largened to the sense,
Shape as part, above man's will,
Of the Imperturbable.

As a prisoner, flight debarred,
Exercising in a yard,
Still retain I, troubled, shaken,
Mean estate, by him forsaken;
And this home, which scarcely took
Impress from his little look
By his faring to the Dim
Grows all eloquent of him.

Housemate, I can think you still
Bounding to the window-sill,
Over which I vaguely see
Your small mound beneath the tree,
Showing in the autumn shade
That you moulder where you played.

THE ACHIEVEMENT OF THE CAT

SAKI

CONFRONT a child, a puppy, and a kitten with sudden danger: the child will turn instinctively for assistance, the puppy will grovel in abject submission to the impending visitation, the kitten will brace its tiny body for a frantic resistance. And dissociate the luxury-loving cat from the atmosphere of social comfort in which it usually contrives to move, and observe it critically under the adverse conditions of civilisation — that civilisation which can impel a man to the degradation of clothing himself in tawdry ribald garments and capering mountebank dances in the street for the earning of the few coins that keep him on the respectable, or non-criminal, side of society. The cat of the slums and alleys, starved, outcast, harried, still keeps amid the prowlings of its adversity the bold, free, panther-tread with which it paced of yore the temple courts of Thebes, still displays the self-reliant watchfulness which man has never taught it to lay aside. And when its shifts and clever managings have not sufficed to stave off inexorable fate, when its enemies have proved too strong or too many for its defensive powers, it dies fighting to the last, quivering with the choking rage of mastered resistance, and voicing in its deathyell that agony of bitter remonstrance which human animals, too, have flung at the powers that may be; the last protest against a destiny that might have made them happy — and has not.

ACKNOWLEDGEMENTS

The publishers wish to thank the copyright holders for permission to include certain material in this volume:

Gyles Brandreth: to Robson Books Ltd for "Pope Innocent VIII Orders Cat Worshippers To Be Burnt As Witches", "Queen Victoria", "Room 8 – The Classroom Cat", and "Mouser and Ratter" from SNIPPETS FROM CATS' TALES by Gyles Brandreth, Robson Books, 1987.

Jill Caravan and Marcus Schneck: to Quarto Plc for "Territorial Cats" from CAT FACTS by Marcus Schneck and Jill Caravan, Stanley Paul.

The Cat: to THE CAT, the official journal of the Cats Protection League for "The Woman's Friend", African Traditional, from THE CAT, The Cats Protection League, 1936, "Fears For My Cat" and "Wartime Cats" from THE CAT, The Cats Protection League, 1942, and for "Clever Cat" from THE CAT, the official journal of the Cats Protection League.

Margaret Ellis: to The Cats Protection League for "Church Cats" by Margaret Ellis from A PASSION FOR CATS edited by Philip Wood, David & Charles, 1987.

Bruce Fogle: to Harvill, an imprint of HarperCollins Publishers Limited for "Ming's Death" from PETS AND THEIR PEOPLE by Bruce Fogle, Harvill, 1983.

Judy Gardiner: to the author and Rupert Crew Limited for "The Death of Grandma" from CAT CHAT by Judy Gardiner (Muller).

David Greene: to Reed Consumer Books for "Cat Enemies", "The Murderous Captain" and "The Trapeze Artist" from INCREDIBLE CATS by David Greene, Methuen, London, 1984.

Geoffrey Household: to Geoffrey Household and Little, Brown and Company for "Abner of the Porch" from SABRES IN THE SAND, Little, Brown and Company, 1959.

Moncrif: to Associated University Presses for "The Lady Who Needed a Cat" translated by Reginald Bretnor from MONCRIF'S CATS, Golden Cockerel Press, 1961.